INVESTIGATING KOLA

A Study of Military Bases using Satellite Photography

£ 3.50

Brassey's titles of related interest

RIES
Finland's Defences

BAXTER
The Soviet Way of Warfare

BELLAMY
Red God of War: Soviet Artillery and Rocket Forces

ERICKSON AND SIMPKIN
The Brainchild of Marshal Tukhachevskii

NIEPOLD
Battle For White Russia

INVESTIGATING KOLA

A Study of Military Bases Using Satellite Photography

by

Tomas Ries

and

Johnny Skorve

BRASSEY'S DEFENCE PUBLISHERS
(a member of the Pergamon Group)

LONDON · OXFORD · WASHINGTON · NEW YORK
BEIJING · FRANKFURT · SÃO PAULO · SYDNEY · TOKYO · TORONTO

U.K. (Editorial)	Brassey's Defence Publishers, 24 Gray's Inn Road, London WC1X 8HR
(Orders)	Brassey's Defence Publishers, Headington Hill Hall, Oxford OX3 0BW, England
U.S.A. (Editorial)	Pergamon-Brassey's International Defense Publishers, 8000 Westpark Drive, 4th Floor, McLean, Virginia 22102, U.S.A.
(Orders)	Pergamon Press, Maxwell House, Fairview Park, Elmsford, New York 10523, U.S.A.
PEOPLE'S REPUBLIC OF CHINA	Pergamon Press, Room 4037, Qianmen Hotel, Beijing, People's Republic of China
FEDERAL REPUBLIC OF GERMANY	Pergamon Press, Hammerweg 6, D-6242 Kronberg, Federal Republic of Germany
BRAZIL	Pergamon Editora, Rua Eça de Queiros, 346, CEP 04011, Paraiso, São Paulo, Brazil
AUSTRALIA	Pergamon-Brassey's Defence Publishers, P.O. Box 544, Potts Point, N.S.W. 2011, Australia
JAPAN	Pergamon Press, 8th Floor, Matsuoka Central Building, 1–7–1 Nishishinjuku, Shinjuku-ku, Tokyo 160, Japan
CANADA	Pergamon Press Canada, Suite No. 271, 253 College Street, Toronto, Ontario, Canada M5T 1R5

Copyright © 1987 Norsk Utenrikspolitisk Institutt

First edition 1987

Library of Congress Cataloging in Publication Data
Ries, Tomas, 1953-
Investigating Kola.
1. Kola Peninsula (R.S.F.S.R.)–Strategic aspects
2. Military bases, Russian–Russian S.F.S.R.–Kola
Peninsula. 3. Space surveillance–United States,
I. Skorve, Johnny, II. Title.
UA778.K65R54   1987   355'.033047'23   87-15086

British Library Cataloguing in Publication Data
Ries, Tomas
Investigating Kola: a study of military
bases using satellite photography.
1. Military bases–Russian S.F.S.R.
Kola Peninsula
I. Title II. Skorve, Johnny
355.7'0947'23   UA770

ISBN 0-08-034755-X

Front cover:
The town of Murmansk and the naval base
of Severomorsk (Photo: NASA, colour
coding: Johnny Skorve)

Printed in Great Britain by A. Wheaton & Co. Ltd., Exeter

Foreword

To interested observers in Norway as well as abroad the presence and also the approximate location of Soviet military forces and bases on the Kola Peninsula has been common knowledge for a long time. This is especially true with respect to naval forces and bases. It has been widely published that nearly fifty per cent of the Soviet submarine force, and more than fifty per cent of the modern Soviet ballistic missile-carrying submarines are based at the Kola Peninsula, mostly in the vicinity of the Murmansk fjord. It is also well-known that there are two motorised infantry divisions with base facilities on the peninsula, one in the north-western part near the border with Norway, and the other further to the south. Several sources have reported the presence of some fifteen to twenty larger airfields on the Kola. More recently, the location of fifteen of these in the central and western part of the peninsula has been reported.

To a large extent, therefore, we know what is on the Kola. This kind of knowledge is, however, abstract in a sense. One unique feature of this study is that by using satellite photographs it displays visually the presence of military installations previously only reported. That may not necessarily contribute to the already established knowledge of their existence there, but it may, nevertheless, add a new and significant dimension to our perception of it.

The use of satellite photographs in this study is not limited to the corroboration of information from other open sources. Close examination of the photographs also provides new information. This is especially true with respect to the exact geographical location, the size, number and configuration, and in some cases also parts of the outfit of military installations on the Kola. Consequently this study presents a lot of information not previously available from open sources. Two discoveries deserve particular mention:

> The construction of a new, very large and till now unreported airfield in the southern part of the peninsula next to the bay of Kandalaksha.

> The exact location of the previously reported new large naval base at Gremikha in the north-eastern part of the Kola, with a rather detailed outline of the base and its inland supporting facilities.

The present study has been made possible by the special competence and knowledge of its two authors.

Tomas Ries is presently engaged at NUPI in a research project on the dynamics and impact of the naval situation in the Norwegian Sea and the North Atlantic. The project is supported financially by the Ford Foundation. The present study is an off-spring from this project. Within the project Ries is extending his studies of Soviet interests and military capabilities relating to Russia's north-western border areas.

Johnny Skorve is a geoscientist who has for several years been working with satellite remote-sensing applications to geoscience, like mapping geological structures, climatological and hydrological studies, mapping of snowlines on glaciers, snow-melting and breaking up of lake ice. His interests also include geomorphology and geology of terrestial moons and planets.

As a part of the Ford Foundation research project and as an introduction to the analysis of the photographs used, Thomas Ries presents an overview of Soviet military interests along her north-western borders (Part I). This includes a broader study of the organisation of Soviet forces, with special reference to the North-western TVD (Theatre of Military Operations), the Arctic, and the North Atlantic, and an outline of the hierarchy of Soviet strategic, operational and tactical interests and objectives in the area. This is interesting for two reasons. It is the first time that the operational combat organisation of the Soviet armed forces has been systematically presented, and it leads to a more structured and revised understanding of the strategic situation in the Nordic area.

As a supplement to the analysis of the photographs in Part II, Johnny Skorve outlines the physical and economic geography of the Kola Peninsula, and gives a brief introduction to the existing civilian photo-satellite technology.

The authors as well as NUPI want to thank the Geographical Institute at the University of Oslo for letting Johnny Skorve use its photograph laboratory for the production of these and other Landsat photographs presented in the study. The front cover, showing the town of Murmansk with the Severomorsk base to its north, has been produced at Kodak Laboratories in Norway.

JOHN KRISTEN SKOGAN*
Oslo, August 1986

*John Kristen Skogan is a senior Researcher in NUPI. He is a specialist in the strategic situation in Europe and of the Soviet Northern Fleet.

Contents

List of Plates

List of Maps

List of Tables and Charts

Part 1

The Soviet Military Operational Command Structure and its Application to Fenno-scandia

TOMAS RIES

Introduction

Map 1 shows the position of the Kola Peninsula from a global perspective. Its relatively sheltered location, northeast of Fenno-scandia and on the edge of the Arctic Ocean, has tended to shield it from daily news coverage. Nonetheless, it is of vital military strategic importance for the Soviet Union and has led to the establishment on the peninsula of the largest military basing complex in the world. This includes two main strategic nuclear submarine bases, two strategic nuclear bomber bases, two strategic early warning and target acquisition radar complexes, about seventy strategic air defence SAM complexes, one theatre nuclear missile launch complex, seven main submarine bases, nine major bases for surface forces, twenty-two main airbases with hardened aircraft shelters and runways exceeding 1,600 metres, eighteen secondary airfields, the prepositioning and deployment infrastructure for one front-level army and very many further installations.[1]

This is the consequence of the geographical location of the Kola Peninsula which makes it an indispensable asset for the prosecution of vital elements of Soviet

© Tomas Ries

MAP 1. The Kola Peninsula and the World

3

military grand strategy. This study examines the role of the Kola in this context. It is divided into two parts. The first part examines why the Kola and adjacent areas are of strategic importance to the Soviet Union, while the second part consists of an empirical study of the actual basing infrastructure of the Kola, based on an analysis of satellite photographs of the area and available open information.

THE STRATEGIC IMPORTANCE OF THE KOLA PENINSULA.

The Soviet Union has deployed important elements of her military forces to the Kola Peninsula, and prepared the infrastructure for the rapid reinforcement of the area by further large military contingents. This involves primary strategic forces, secondary theatre-level forces, and tertiary front-level forces, whose deployment, and organisation for wartime operations, is closely interlinked. Much of the first part of this study is based upon an examination of the type and quantity of these forces on the Kola. The purpose is partly to familiarise the reader with the forces actually deployed to the area, but is mainly designed to explain the significance of this deployment. For the type of military forces based on the Kola provides both important clues as to the Soviet strategic perception of the importance of this entire area, as well as constituting in themselves one of the main determinants of the strategic climate of northern and central Fenno-scandia. As such, an understanding of their role in Soviet strategy is an important element in understanding the dangers facing what we have become accustomed to, misleadingly understand as 'Nordic stability'.

For the implications of the Soviet deployment of certain types and quantities of military forces in the Kola area to be grasped it is first necessary to gain some understanding of the role and nature of the various branches of the Soviet armed forces within Soviet military strategy. Therefore, before making a more thorough presentation of the types and relative numbers of forces allocated to the Kola, this study will first outline the operational organisation of the Soviet armed forces, followed by an outline of the organisation of northern Europe within Soviet operational military planning. This will provide the groundwork for the subsequent analysis of the implications of the actual Soviet deployment pattern to the Kola.

CHAPTER 1

The Kola and the Operational Organisation of the Soviet Armed Forces

The importance of the Kola is derived from the fact that it is geographically well placed for the prosecution of Soviet global nuclear strategy, and has led to the basing of key elements of the strategic nuclear forces on the Peninsula. This is probably the single most important factor for the strategic importance of the Peninsula, and the main driving force behind the general buildup of Soviet forces in the area. It has in turn led to deployment to the area of a number of additional theatre-level forces, whose primary purpose is the protection of the strategic assets. While portions of these forces can be assigned a limited number of additional theatre-level missions, such as cutting NATO central Atlantic SLOC, this is strictly subject to the requirements of the primary strategic defence responsibilities. Finally, a number of tertiary front level forces are assigned to the Kola area, responsible for supporting the theatre-level forces in their strategic support tasks.

From a functional point of view there are therefore three types of Soviet forces deployed on the Kola Peninsula.

Primary global strategic nuclear forces, with an extra-regional orientation but whose presence is the main determinant of the strategic importance of the Kola.

Secondary theatre-level nuclear and conventional forces, with a clear regional orientation, charged with the defence and support of the strategic forces.

Tertiary frontal forces, with a local regional orientation, charged with the support of the operational forces in the execution of their primary strategic support task.

To understand the strategic and military operational environment of the Kola the existence of, and causal relationship between, these types of Soviet military objectives and associated forces must be clear. For the forces placed on the Kola are there for specific reasons, and these reasons can only be discerned if we are able to place the deployed military forces in the context of Soviet grand strategy. This applies equally to the smallest naval infantry brigade in Petsamo and Murmansk as it does for the strategically vital SSBN forces based at Polyarnyy and environs. They, and all other forces in the area, are part of a greater strategy. To see how the Kola, and therefore all of north-central Fenno-scandia, fits into this it is necessary to see the separate military forces from this broader perspective before examining their specific roles. To examine the various military units in isolation is as meaningless as it is misleading if we are trying to study their role in Soviet regional military planning.

Secondly, it is only by looking at the various elements of the Soviet armed forces from the perspective of their role in Soviet overall strategy and military operational thinking that we can presume at all to categorise them into such units as Fleets, 'Ground Forces' and so on. For it is this type of operational organisation which more accurately reflects Soviet military strategy than the peacetime administrative organisation of forces. Thus it is very misleading, if we are to understand Soviet military strategy, operations and objectives, to think of the Soviet armed forces in terms of Strategic Rocket Forces, Ground Forces, Aerospace Defence Forces, Air Forces or the Navy. These organisations exist, but with the exception of the first and third services listed, only as administrative entities, grouped together primarily for logistical purposes. They have nothing to do with the operational organisation or wartime use of Soviet forces, do not have their own independent commands and do not operate as a single cohesive body. Instead there exists an entirely separate operational command structure which groups together elements of the five administrative services in combat task forces specially tailored for their military assignments. It is these operational commands, and the combined arms combat forces which they direct, which reflect actual Soviet operational military thinking, and from which perspective it is therefore vital to see the Kola deployments.

The Organisation of the Soviet Armed Forces.

The organisation of the Soviet armed forces is by no means as clear as it is sometimes laid out to be. In fact the Soviet military exists as two parallel but separate and entirely distinct organisations. The one is responsible for the administration and housekeeping of the armed forces, while the second is responsible for operations and combat. The first builds and maintains while the second uses and disposes.

This is not generally recognised in the West and so far, with few exceptions[2], there has not been any attempt to focus specifically on this distinction. However it is vital, as it is the latter organisation which shows us how the Soviet forces are actually grouped for combat operations, and provides us with the key indicators as to how they are to be used. It is also important because, once the relative ranking of the various combined combat commands within the overall command structure hierarchy is clear, it permits us to draw conclusions about Soviet strategic priorities. When we compare this to the actual regional deployment of Soviet forces we are able to arrive at a rough idea of the strategic, operational and tactical value of this given region within Soviet overall strategy.

The Administrative and Housekeeping Organisation.

Table 1.1 shows the administrative and housekeeping organisation of the Soviet Armed Forces.[3] This is the classical representation of the Soviet military as it has usually been presented in the West. In this form it consists of five services which, in their order of importance, are listed as:[4]

The Strategic Rocket Forces.
The Ground Forces.
The Aerospace Defence Forces.
The Air Forces.
The Navy.

In addition there is the detached arm of service:

The Airborne Forces.[5]

Each of these six commands contains all the forces of that particular type (eg all ground forces under the Ground Forces Service, all naval forces under the Navy). These are listed in the table under the service headings. Each of the six services is commanded by a Commander in Chief (CINC) of that particular service,[6] who in turn, via the General Staff, is subordinated to the Ministry of Defence.[7] The Airborne Forces, though not constituting a full service in themselves, are considered an independent Arm of Service, with their own CINC and in peacetime subordinated directly to the Ministry of Defence[8] via the General Staff.[a]

This presentation of the Soviet Armed Forces is highly misleading for two reasons. Firstly, because it could easily give the impression that all the forces of a

---

(a) See Appendix I. *Terminology: Soviet Administrative Commands.* for a more complete treatment of Soviet administrative command terms.

TABLE 1.1. Administrative and Housekeeping Organisation of the Soviet Armed Forces.

given service are commanded by the CINC of that particular service, who therefore appears to have considerable operational importance. Nothing could be further from the truth. This organisation tells us absolutely nothing about the actual operational use of the various elements of the Soviet Armed Forces. It is purely and only an administrative grouping of forces, where the composition of the units is almost entirely a function of logistic convenience. Of the five CINCs it is only two – the CINC Strategic Rocket Forces and the CINC Vojska PVO – which have both administrative and operational command of their forces. The remaining three CINCs are purely administrative commanders, and have a relatively low military rank, with very little to say about the actual combat use of their respective forces.[9] Within the operational command structure, at the most they may provide advice to the Supreme Command (VGK), but only if requested to do so by the VGK.[10] Thus in terms of the combat organisation of the Soviet Armed Forces this housekeeping command structure is totally irrelevant. It is important to note that the same applies to the Military Districts which, though they do reflect more accurately the wartime geographical planning of the Soviet Union, serve only as administrative and logistic support organisations for the operational commands.[11] They are responsible for the upkeep and training of the armed forces within their district, but for the use of these forces they hand them over to the special regional operational commands which exist independently for this purpose. In wartime, for instance, the Headquarters and staff of the Leningrad Military District would continue to function, tasked with the supply and logistic support of all forces in this area. It would be only one of many commands subordinated to the Arctic Detached Front Headquarters, which in peacetime consists of a special command staff located near Leningrad. The Leningrad Military District HQ, located in Leningrad in peacetime, therefore has nothing to do with the operational wartime command of the military forces within the Leningrad MD.

Secondly, the peacetime housekeeping organisation is misleading in that it implies that all the military forces within a particular Service have the same general ranking within Soviet strategy as that service; thus, for instance, that all Navy units rank as fifth and least important in the military hierarchy. Again, nothing could be further from the truth. There are branches of the Navy, such as the SSBN forces, which for administrative reasons are classed as part of the Navy, but in operational terms are part of the strategic 'Strategic Nuclear Forces' command, which is indisputably the most important operational Soviet military service. Thus this portion of the 'Navy' is among the most highly prioritised in Soviet strategy, while other elements, such as the Amphibious Assault Forces, fall under the relatively more lowly operational

strategic Front commands, or even under the operational level Army commands. The same principle, as shall be outlined in more detail below, applies to every one of the five administrative military organisations. Thus also in terms of the strategic priority accorded to the various components of the Soviet armed forces this peacetime housekeeping organisation is completely irrelevant. This is serious because unless we have an understanding of the strategic priority of the various Soviet military operational commands, the logic of their deployment and use, and the subsequent regional deployment implications cannot be understood.

It is therefore important to be aware of the fact that there are two military organisations in the Soviet Union, one dealing with administration, while the second is in charge of operations. It is the second which we must use when examining Soviet regional military interests on the basis of her deployed forces.

This dichotomy exists for two principal reasons. Partly because the actual prosecution of military operations calls for highly integrated combined arms operations, where elements from several different services must cooperate very closely. It is therefore far more rational to establish operational commands with subordinated forces tailored to the mission of that command, and not determined by crude service criteria, and also because in Soviet strategic planning different operational objectives have different priorities. Therefore a far more nuanced command structure hierarchy, tailored to strategic planning priorities, is required than that which exists in the simplified logistically based housekeeping organisation. Each of these two points will be dealt with in turn below.

The Operational and Combat Organisation.

Table 1.2.(A) shows the way in which the five administrative commands translate into the operational command structure. The administrative commands are shown on the left side of the table, while the actual combat commands are shown on the right. All of the strategic level combat commands are included (one Supreme Command (VGK), six Commanders-in-Chief (GK) and seven Commanders (K)) but only one Front and Fleet are depicted, due to lack of space. In actual fact each Commander-in-Chief of a Theatre of Strategic Military Action (GK TVD) would have several fronts, as well as further subordinate commands, such as Spetsnaz brigades, Military District logistic commands, etc. The exact composition is tailored to the local conditions and requirements. However, the point of this table is not to provide a complete outline of all Soviet existing commands, but rather to illustrate the way in which the administrative services split up into integrated combat commands.

TABLE 1.2.(A). The Relationship of the Soviet Military Housekeeping Organisation to the Operational Organisation.

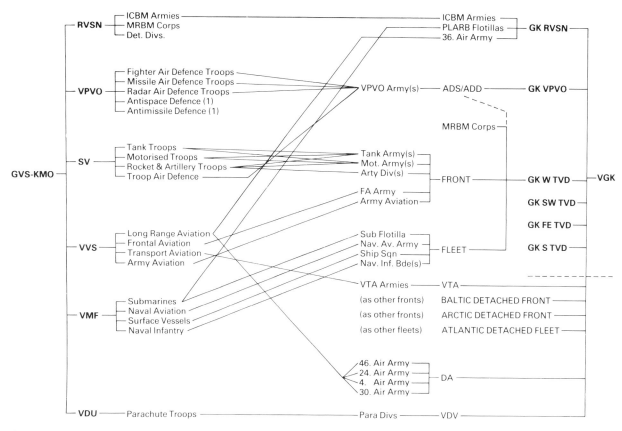

© Tomas Ries

This translation from administrative to operational command structure is due to the fact that none of the five administrative services (with the exception of the Strategic Air Defence Forces, and to a more limited extent the Strategic Rocket Forces) could achieve any meaningful military objectives on their own. For the Soviet Union to pursue her primary global nuclear strategic objectives the forces incorporated in the service of the Strategic Rocket Forces are not enough. Their particular characteristics and advantages must be integrated with the special qualities and capabilities of the submarine-based intercontinental range strategic nuclear missiles and the special qualities of the intercontinental range strategic nuclear bombers. Therefore for the operational prosecution of Soviet global nuclear strategy these three nuclear branches have been combined under one single strategic command. This incorporates all 'Strategic Nuclear Forces' with the three ICBM Armies, two SSBN Flotillas and the 36 Aviation Army under its absolute operational command. This strategic command also has the highest priority in Soviet strategic planning, and its Commander-in-Chief is second only to the Supreme Commander himself. (See pages 10 and 25 for more details.) This also means that the forces it commands are of primary importance to the Soviet Union. As is outlined later in this study this has

considerable significance for Kola and all of north-central Fenno-scandia.

This need for integrated combined operational commands, with a specially tailored mix of various branches of the Soviet Armed Forces applies to all levels of the Soviet military as is illustrated in the table. Thus, on a far lower level, a ground offensive cannot be carried out only by ground forces. Instead very close interaction between for instance frontal aviation, army aviation, ground forces, perhaps theatre nuclear weapons and parachute divisions, as well as in certain areas naval amphibious units – to mention but a few of the various forces – is required. Therefore special combined TVD and Front commands exist, which have immediate and integrated control of these forces and can be allocated further forces if required from higher commands.

As a result it is highly inconvenient to have separate operational commands based on an artificial service criteria. Instead the forces are grouped for combat according to their function, under combined service commands, each of which is responsible for achieving certain military objectives ranging from the frontal level, the theatre level and up to the global strategic level. It is therefore this organisation of the Soviet military which provides us with an idea of the Soviet use of military force as well as the relative hierarchy of the various commands.

The actual combat and operational organisation of the Soviet Armed Forces is shown on Table 1.2.(B). The purpose of the table is to illustrate the principles of the operational command structure and not to give a complete (which would fill several pages) outline of all Soviet combat commands down to the tactical level. Therefore only the strategic level commands are given completely, while the Front and Fleet depicted are representative. However specific details of the Front, Army Fleet and Corps commands of the Arctic Front in the North-western TVD and the Baltic Detached Front and Northern Front of the GK Western TVD are provided in a later section.

Details of the functioning of Soviet combat command systems are provided in a number of publications[12] and will not be dealt with specifically here. Instead only the main characteristics of Soviet High Commands will be covered, to place them in relation to each other.

The Supreme Commander.(VGK)

There is one Supreme Command (VGK) [(b)] which, with its support group (Stavka VGK) and assisted by the General Staff (GS) is in absolute command of all forces. These are in turn commanded by six Commanders-in-Chief (GK) and at least seven Commanders (K) all of whom are under the direct command of the VGK.[13] In addition under certain conditions the VGK can appoint special Commanders-in-Chief assigned to

---

(b) See Appendix II. *Terminology: Soviet Operational Commands* for a more complete treatment of Soviet operational command terms.

assist a command which is responsible for a particularly important strategic operation.[14]

The Six Commanders-in-Chief.(GK)

The operational forces commanded by the six Commanders-in-Chief (GK) can be divided into two basic types:[15]

The two strategic nuclear commands. Under the two GK commanding the two services responsible for implementing Soviet nuclear strategic objectives. (GK SNF and GK VPVO).

The four territorial TVD commands. Under the four GK commanding the four operational integrated TVD Headquarters presently established in peacetime. (GK WTVD, GK SWTVD, GK FETVD and GK STVD).

Of the two types it is fairly certain that the two strategic nuclear related GK have the highest priority. They command respectively the 'offensive' arm of Soviet nuclear strategy (GK Strategic Nuclear Forces) and the 'defensive' arm (GK Vojska PVO). This is dealt with in more detail on pages 10 and 19.

Below them are the territorial TVD related GK. They have very powerful forces under their command tailored to their missions and the conditions of their operational area. Thus the GK Western TVD commands four Fronts, one Group of Tank Armies, one Fleet, one MRBM Corps and has operational command links to the Vojska PVO and integrated Warsaw Pact Air Defence Sectors in his theatre. He is also in direct command of a number of smaller and more specialised combat formations, such as Spetsnaz brigades, as well as the numerous branches of the support services. In addition the Stavka VGK can allocate for his use at least two theatre bomber Aviation

TABLE 1.2.(B). Operational and Combat Organisation of the Soviet Armed Forces.

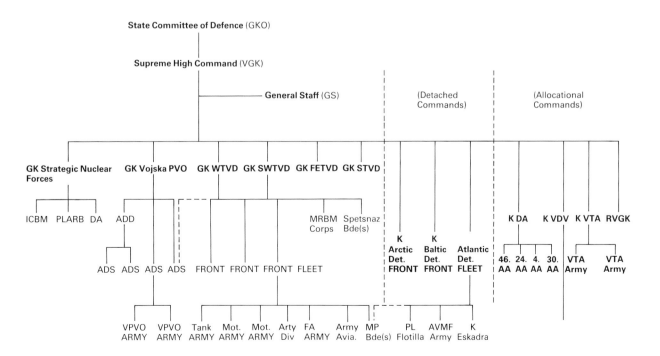

Armies, between three and seven Airborne Divisions, the entire force of the Military Transport Aviation, and other smaller specialised forces. On the next step down each of his Fronts in turn commands a varying number of Tank and Motorised Armies, special frontal artillery formations (including nuclear launchers), one Frontal Aviation Army, and further specific formations, such as amphibious assault forces, according to their requirements. The exact number and type of these formations vary considerably from one Front to another. Details of the specific organisation of the Northern, Baltic Detached and Arctic Detached Fronts are provided on page 21.

At this point, it is probably also useful to note in passing, the distinction between the concept of the TVD as a military command entity (eg GK WTVD) and the concept of the TVD as a theatre of strategic military action (TVD). The first constitutes an actual active strategic-level military command headquarters with full command links to all operational military units within that TVD with the exception of the special Stavka VGK detached commands. The Soviets have at present, according to open sources, only the four operational High Commands of a TVD mentioned above.[16] These are active and operational command headquarters, presently either commanding ongoing military operations (eg GK STVD in Afghanistan) or ready at any time to assume operational command of all military forces in that TVD for the conduct of integrated theatre level military operations.

On the other hand Soviet strategic planners have divided the whole world into up to sixteen TVDs,[17] which cover every part of the earth's surface. These consist of territorial entities, considered by Soviet strategic planners to form a cohesive territory for the prosecution of military action on a strategic scale. As such it is purely a territorial designation, and does not imply that any special theatre level command headquarters, or special integrated theatre level combat formations, exist for that TVD.

As a consequence it is important to note that while the concept of the North-western TVD as an area for military action on a strategic scale (see section 1.3) in all likelihood exists, it is almost certain that no specific GK NWTVD, as a command system with prepared combined operational military formations for theatre operations, exists.[18] This does of course not mean that military forces in the NWTVD do not exist, nor that they are not organised for integrated combined arms regional operations, but it does – as is indicated in the next section immediately below – say a great deal about the Soviet understanding of the role of these military forces in the NWTVD. We shall return to this point below.

The seven Commanders under direct Stavka VGK command.

In addition to the six main GK commands the VGK also has under his direct command seven Commanders (K). These control two basic types of forces:

Detached Fronts and Fleets. These operate directly under the Stavka VGK command without an intermediate GK command. This is so for a variety of reasons, some of which is dealt with in more depth on pages 22 and 23. There are at least three such detached commands, all of those listed here being directly associated with the Fenno-scandia area.

Allocational commands. These consist of important forces with, in all cases but one, a high mobility. They include the four theatre bomber armies of the DA (K DA), the seven parachute divisions of the Airborne Forces (K VDV), the aircraft armies of the military transport aviation (K VTA), and the strategic reserves (K RVGK). These are retained under the Stavka VGK command, permitting him to allocate portions or all of them to that particular TVD, Front or even Army command which the VGK judges appropriate.

These are lower ranking commands than the six GK but are retained under direct VGK control for two main reasons. In the case of the detached Front and Fleet commands it is because the particular forces listed here are directly involved with the defence of vital Soviet strategic nuclear forces. Therefore their campaigns must be very closely monitored by the Stavka VGK, and their operational direction and support requirements given particular attention at the highest level. This applies directly to the Northern Fleet and the Arctic Detached Front. The Baltic Detached Front on the other hand constitutes a so called 'swing asset' whose forces, depending upon the Stavka VGK evaluation of the overall strategic situation, could be assigned either to the Arctic Detached Front, or for independent Front Operations against and through Sweden, or could be assigned to the Northern Front of the Western TVD to support the attack against the Danish Straits. There are other reasons for the detached special status of the forces facing northern and central Fenno-scandia, but these are dealt with in more detail on pages 19 to 21.

The more detailed combat organisation of the forces facing northern Europe is provided on pages 19 to 21. The important point at this stage, now that the general Soviet operational military command structure has been outlined, is to note the hierarchy of the various commands, and their ranking relationship to each other. This is dealt with in the separate section below.

The Hierarchy of Soviet Operational Commands.

Like any other country, the Soviet Union has military objectives which have differing priorities within her overall strategy. Thus for instance deterrence of, and defence against, a strategic nuclear attack, is a more important strategic objective than the prosecution of military operations in central Europe. The latter is important, but only if the first is assured. If not, the latter loses all meaning. As a result the command responsible for the strategic nuclear objectives, and the forces within this command, have a higher priority than the command and forces responsible for central European military operations.[19] In a similar vein the neutralisation and occupation of, for instance, the Baltic Straits is an important Soviet military wartime objective, but is primarily a function of its contribution to the main military operations against central Europe and the United Kingdom. Therefore in this case also the command responsible for wartime operations against Danish territory (under the Commander, Northern Front) is subordinated to the higher command responsible for all of central Europe (under the Commander-in-Chief, Western TVD).

As a result there are different levels of Soviet military commands, each roughly reflecting the priority of that command's responsibilities within Soviet overall strategy. Table 1.3 shows the Soviet operational command hierarchy.[20] The various commands are listed under the *Command Level* column and include all levels of Soviet operational commands from the Strategic to the highest Tactical level (Division). Each is placed in the context of the type of forces commanded and the geographic scope of that command level's operations. As a general rule, the more destructive forces a command has subordinated to it and the larger the geographic scope of the operations it can command (with the exception of the special

allocated GK of a major strategic effort), the more important, and the more highly prioritised, that command is. This is also reflected in the position of each of the listed command levels within the levels of Soviet Military Art.[21] These are listed on the far left of the table alongside the numbered ranking of the nine levels.[(c)] When we look closer at the forces on the Kola this hierarchical relationship will be of significance.

Strategic level commands.

There are seven such commands established at present, but the number can vary, both in peacetime (as when the fourth operational TVD command and the GK Southern TVD, were added in the late 70s to manage the Afghanistan operation) and in wartime, when additional territorial GK TVDs can be established and the Stavka VGK can appoint special GKs to manage certain specific strategically vital operations.

For reasons noted earlier it is likely that the GK of the Strategic Nuclear Forces (GK SNF) is the most important of all the Soviet High Commands.[22] This is also borne out by a number of official Soviet sources.

(c) It is important to note that from now on whenever the terms 'Strategic', 'Operational' and so forth are used written with a capital letter the reference is to the Soviet concept.

TABLE 1.3. The Operational Command Hierarchy of the Soviet Armed Forces.

Level in Soviet Military Art	Rank	Command Level		Geographic Scope	Operational Orientation	Forces Commanded
STRATEGY	①	VGK		Global	Strategic Global	All Soviet and allied military forces.
	②	GK	GK SNF GK VPVO	Global	Strategic Global, Nuclear	All intercontinental nuclear forces. All strategic aerospace forces.
	③	GK		Front/Corps	Main Strategic Direction	All forces participating in the strategic operation plus VGK allocational commands.
	④	GK	GK WTVD, GK SWTVD, GK FETVD, GK STVD.	TVD	Strategic Direction	All forces within that TVD.
OPERATIONAL-STRATEGIC	⑤	K	K DA, K VDV, K VTA, K RVGK.	Decisive targets	Main Strategic Direction/ Strategic Direction	All the forces within the respective allocational command.
	⑥	K		Front	Front	All front-level forces.
OPERATIONAL	⑦	n.a.		Army/Fleet	Army/Fleet	All army/fleet level forces.
OPERATIONAL-TACTICAL	⑧	n.a.		Army Corps	Army Corps	All corps forces
TACTICAL	⑨	n.a.		Division	Division	All divisional forces.

In his 1982 book, *Always in Readiness to Defend the Fatherland*, Marshall Ogarkov wrote:[23]

> The chief component of (our) power in present-day conditions are the strategic nuclear forces, which serve as the basic factor deterring the aggressor and which have the capability, in case the aggressor unleashes a war with the use of nuclear weapons . . . of immediately carrying out a crushing retaliatory strike. Launches of modern land and sea-based ballistic missiles are automated.

This message is repeated in numerous authoritative texts. And the logic is quite clear. Should the GK SNF be unable to deter a nuclear attack on the Soviet Union all the other commands become relatively meaningless. In addition, and as the Soviets often stress, this is the only command able to strike directly at the enemy capability of waging war and capable of threatening the enemy's very existence. Therefore this command has a priority over all others, probably closely followed by the strategic air defence forces (GK VPVO) which – to some extent assisted by the GK SNF – has the main responsibility for frustrating an enemy strategic nuclear attack on the Soviet Union.[24] Therefore the VPVO also has an independent GK, which has received a very high allocation of economic resources for its task.[25]

On the next step down in the command hierarchy come the GKs of the TVDs. They also command enormous power, but this is basically limited to the theatre level. While this includes important nuclear forces these on the whole do not have the capacity for, and almost certainly are not intended for, any strategic intercontinental operations. Nor could these commands in any way manage the strategic nuclear relationship with the main nuclear power threatening the Soviet Union, ie the United States. Therefore these TVD commands are on a lower command level than the strategic nuclear commands.

However on the theatre level they are the most powerful commands in the Soviet military which, with the exception of the special detached front and service commands retained directly under the Stavka VGK (see below), command all theatre nuclear and conventional forces of the Soviet military. The priority amongst the GK TVD can vary depending upon circumstances and upon which geographic region receives the brunt of Soviet strategic attention. It appears quite certain that at almost all times the GK of the Western Strategic Direction has the first priority, which is clearly indicated by the number and quality of the forces under his command. However if the VGK were to decide to allocate as his representative a GK to manage a Main Strategic Operation, this could receive absolute priority.

Operational–Strategic Commands.

All of the above commands fall under the category of 'Strategic' in the definition of Soviet Military Art.[26] On the next level down are the 'Operational-Strategic'

operations. These probably include two command levels, with the Commanders of the special detached Operational-Strategic forces under the direct command of the Stavka VGK (K DA, K VDV, K VTA and K RVGK) ranking higher than the Front commands under the various TVD GKs, and the detached Front Commands under direct Stavka VGK control (K).[27]

Operational Commands and Lower.

The next command level downwards contains the 'Operational' commands, which includes all Army and Fleet commands subordinated to the Operational-Strategic Front commands.[28] This is significant because, as we shall see on pages 19 to 21, it helps place the role of the 'Northern Fleet' – ie the Kola based naval forces *minus* the SSBN forces carrying intercontinental range SLBMs – in context.

On the next step down we have the 'Operational-Tactical' formations, consisting of Army Corps units.[29] These are relatively rare in the Soviet armed forces, but it is worth noting that two such formations exist as part of the Arctic Detached Front. Again, this provides interesting clues as to the Soviet operational view of north-central Fenno-scandia. (See section 1.3.). On the lowest level in this table are the tactical commands, which include all those from the divisional level and downwards.[30]

The importance of the above outline is that it now permits us to place the military forces deployed by the Soviet Union in context, both by providing a means of grouping them into their operational formations, and by placing these formations in their role and 'rank' within Soviet overall strategy. Thus the High Command formations, and the operations of these forces (as well as their protection) have, generally speaking the highest priority, while the next level of command and their forces have the next highest, and so forth. When we now look at the Soviet military forces deployed to the Nordic area we can group them into their operational formations. From this we can see which type of command they belong to, which in turn provides us with the all important clues as to the Soviet perception of the military use of that area.

Armed with these basic working tools we can now take a closer look at the place of Fenno-scandia within Soviet overall strategy and subsequently at the North-western TVD and especially of the main basing area in this TVD, the Kola peninsula.

FENNO-SCANDIA IN SOVIET MILITARY PLANNING.

Before examining the Kola and adjacent areas specifically it is worth placing all of the north-western Soviet Union and thereby north-central Fennoscandia, in context. This consists of determining which primary Soviet military strategic interests are located in or adjacent to the Nordic region. This can be done by examining which Strategic level commands (GKs) have important interests (in the form of deployed forces or military-political objectives) in the area. These in turn give rise to secondary regional objectives under Operational-Strategic commands (Fronts), whose forces, and in some cases the commands themselves, again can be identified. These in turn give rise to even lower level regional wartime military objectives, which are the responsibility of the local Operational commands (Armies and Fleets) whose forces also can be identified. Within this general framework the main regional objectives and missions of all of these forces can be assessed. The following three sections will seek to do this.

Fenno-Scandia and Soviet Strategic Commands.

Map 1.1 shows Fenno-scandia in the greater context as part of the European TVD and Arctic and Atlantic OTVDs. When we take into account the type of forces deployed by the Soviet Union in the area covered by the map, and place these forces in the context of the operational command structure

hierarchy outlined earlier, it becomes clear that Fenno-scandia itself does not fall under any of the higher Strategic level commands, but is flanked by two main areas of vital strategic importance to the Soviet Union. These are:

The Arctic, which is simultaneously a vital part of the GK SNF Strategic level command and the GK VPVO Strategic level command, both of which are higher ranking commands than the GK WTVD.

Central Western Europe, which is part of the GK WTVD Strategic level command.

Each of these will be dealt with in turn below.

The Arctic OTVD

The Arctic OTVD is of vital concern to the GK SNF and GK VPVO, both of which are the second ranking Strategic level commands in the Soviet command hierarchy. However unlike Western Europe which is an area where the whole of the fourth ranking GK WTVD command focuses its efforts upon, the Arctic only plays a role for part of the GK SNF and GK VPVO forces and interests. However this part is very big and probably makes the Arctic of equal, if not greater, importance to Soviet overall strategic planning than Western Europe.

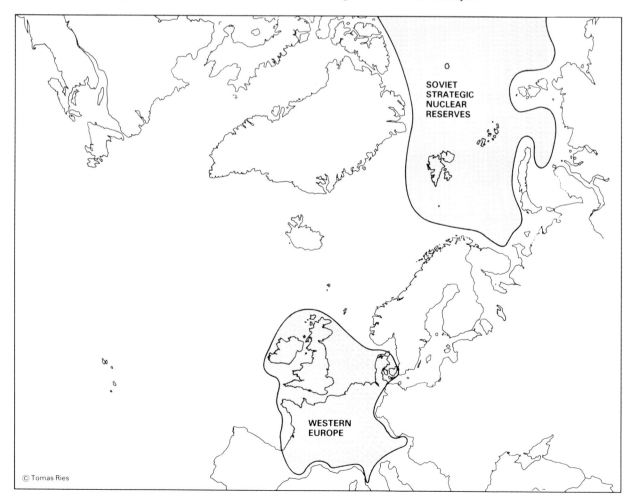

MAP 1.1. Fenno-Scandia and Soviet primary strategic interests in adjacent areas.

For the GK SNF the Arctic is important in that it is the main basing and particular operating area for the Soviet strategic SSBNs, with roughly 66 per cent of the force deployed here. This constitutes two thirds of the Soviet strategic nuclear reserve force and roughly thirty per cent of the total Soviet nuclear arsenal. A more detailed examination of the composition of this force and the rationale for its deployment to the Kola is provided on pages 26 to 28. The important point to note at present being that the protection of this primary strategic nuclear force probably ranks as one of the main priorities of the Soviet strategic planners.

In addition the Arctic plays a major role for the intercontinental strategic bombers of the 36 Aviation Army. A large portion of these would have to transit this area to reach their strategic targets in North America. However this branch of the GK SNF is relatively small, with only 6.7 per cent of total launch platforms and 8.8 per cent of the total equivalent megatonnage (EMT). However this may change in the coming years. Again, the reader is referred to pages 28 and 29 for details.

For the GK VPVO the Arctic constitutes the main forward air defence zone against US strategic bombers, and especially the area facing the Kola–Arkhangelsk–Novaya Zemlya sector is vital in that this constitutes one of the main nuclear strike flightpaths of the US strategic nuclear bomber force. Although there has been a tendency among researchers to focus on US ICBM and SLBM M forces, the threat of the bomber leg of the triad should not be underestimated. Though it only contains 9.9 per cent of the total number of US strategic launch platforms, it carries more nuclear megatonnage than either of the other two services, with 38.5 per cent of the total. Further details are provided on pages 30 to 32, but for the moment it is enough to note that it is almost certain that defence against this force ranks very high in Soviet strategic planning. In addition the Arctic coastline is important to the GK VPVO in that it lies beneath, and as far forward as possible, to the incoming flight paths of US ICBMs, and thus is suitably located for the positioning of strategic Early Warning radars and target acquisition and tracking radars for the Moscow ADD ABM system.

The GK Western TVD

Central Western Europe is, as noted earlier, part of the 'fourth level' Strategic command GK WTVD, which, as noted, is the most important TVD command of the four. This is so for a number of reasons. In peacetime the mere existence of the Western states in the immediate vicinity of the Soviet empire constitutes a constant threat to the legitimacy of the Soviet system, as the relative wealth and affluence of the Western societies put the poor performance of the

Soviet economic and social system to shame. At the same time the democratic freedom of the Western states contrasts sharply with the oppression of the population of Eastern Europe and the Baltic States. Thus defence against this threat to the legitimacy of the Soviet system ranks high in Soviet peacetime priorities. This is noticeable in the caging-in of the population of Eastern Europe behind the elaborate border barriers and the considerable efforts made, in violation of the CSCE agreements, to block the free flow of information from West to East.

In wartime, the neutralisation of Western Europe is important for two main reasons. On the one hand it presents a primary strategic nuclear threat to the Soviet military and civilian heartland west of the Urals. This is because a large number of theatre nuclear weapons are stationed here, and although NATO doctrine primarily calls for their use against military targets when the Soviet conventional superiority threatens to overwhelm NATO defences, many have the capacity of reaching targets as far east as Moscow. From the Soviet point of view this must constitute an unacceptable threat both to Soviet military forces and to the industrial and demographic centres, the bulk of which are covered by the European stationed theatre nuclear systems. Therefore the neutralisation of the nuclear forces stationed in Western Europe at an early stage of any war must rank as one of the prime Soviet strategic priorities. Secondly, it is in Western Europe that the main theatre-level 'conventional' military threat faces the Soviet Union, in the form of the NATO conventional military forces stationed and prepared for operations here. This again provides a powerful incentive for military operations to neutralise these forces in the event of war.

From this perspective the western European part of the GK WTVD poses a constant strategic threat to the legitimacy of the Soviet system, a strategic nuclear threat to the Soviet heartland and the major theatre military threat. As such the long term neutralisation of the threat to Soviet legitimacy and of the theatre military threat, and the rapid neutralisation of the nuclear forces in the event of war, must rank high in Soviet planning.

The important point to note at this stage is however that for the Soviet Union the main strategic centres of gravity in the vicinity of Fenno-scandia lie in Western Europe and in the Arctic. In this sense Fenno-scandia and the north Atlantic do not constitute primary strategic objectives *per se*, but only acquire their importance as a function of their relationship to the Arctic interests of the GK SNF and GK VPVO, and the central European interests of the GK WTVD.

Fenno-Scandia and Soviet secondary strategic support operations.

This is illustrated in Map 1.2 which shows the two main theatre-level strategic support operations which

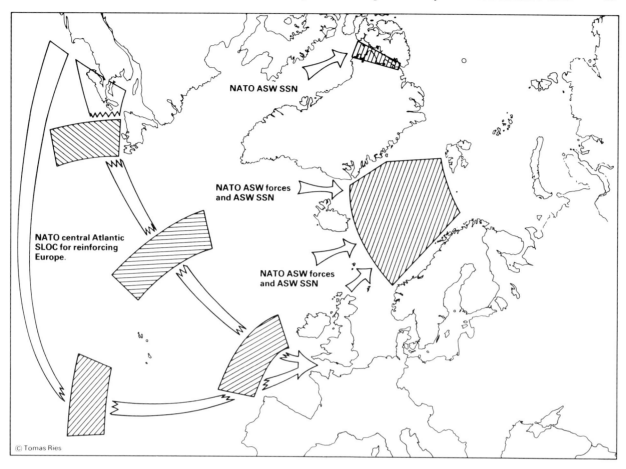

MAP 1.2. Fenno-Scandia and Soviet secondary strategic support operations.

would take place involving forces adjacent to Fenno-scandia and which are required to assist the Soviet forces and efforts in the two focal strategic areas. These are:

For the GK SNF: Defence of the SSBN Arctic hiding and basing areas. This involves Northern Fleet operations to prevent Western ASW forces from reaching the Arctic, through the establishment of in-depth layered naval defensive operations in the Norwegian Sea, and long range submarine based ASW and anti-shipping operations in the Atlantic, directed against NATO military vessels.

For the GK VPVO: The rapid establishment in the Arctic of forward air support bases, radar stations and SAM stations. These would have to be placed as far to the north as possible, and would be especially vital for the IA PVO.

For the GK WTVD: Using the Northern Fleet long range anti-shipping forces in the naval aviation army and submarine flotilla to cut off NATO central Atlantic sea-lines-of-communication (SLOC), thereby preventing the bulk of NATO's conventional military power from reaching the European and North-western TVDs. This involves sea-denial operations by submarines and naval aviation in the central Atlantic, directed against NATO merchant vessels.

These are of course not the only theatre-level strategic support missions which these three Strategic commands would require. Thus the GK WTVD would, in addition to the central Atlantic mission, require theatre bombing operations by the medium-range Aviation Armies, airborne operations, etc., but these would only marginally affect Fenno-scandia. The operations listed above are those two main support operations which involve major theatre level military operations next to Fenno-scandia and which would have major repercussions on the nordic region.

It is also important to note that the GK VPVO support requirement, while very important, would only require a relatively minor military operation. This is mainly because those land and ice areas suitable for the establishment of forward air defence bases are relatively weakly defended or not defended at all. Thus one of the main targets, Svalbard, could be controlled with minimal use of force. Using special forces, the key targets on the islands could probably be controlled within hours, after which regular forces could be flown and shipped in to build up the Soviet combat infrastructure. With an established Soviet population in Barentsburg twice as large as the Norwegian population on the islands, an independent helicopter fleet, permanent representatives at the air-field at Longyearbyen, the lack of Norwegian special forces units on the islands, and so forth, the success of such a venture is virtually guaranteed, and would involve a very small, if highly specialised, military effort.

The same applies to other potential land areas, such as the east coast of Greenland. However attempts to establish fixed air defence support bases here are unlikely since this area, unlike Svalbard, is difficult to defend against NATO conventional counter-attacks with special forces and/or air attack. Far more likely would be attempts to establish dispersed minimum FOL on the Arctic ice itself. These operations as well would involve a minimum military effort, and mainly call for skilled engineers and a flexible and mobile air support system.

Though these GK VPVO Arctic strategic support operations would involve small military forces they are nonetheless vitally important to Soviet strategic planning. This is largely due to the introduction since 1982 of the AGM-86B Air Launched Cruise Missile (ALCM) in the US strategic bomber arsenal. With an approximate range of 2,400 kilometres and, at present, a very limited Soviet capability to intercept the ALCM once launched, this has meant that the US strategic bombers now have to be intercepted and shot down before they have launched their ALCMs. This has created a very urgent need for forward airbases for the IA PVO fighters to give them the range for such extended Arctic intercept operations.

However, the major large scale theatre level strategic support operations affecting Fenno-scandia involve the Norwegian Sea and North Atlantic (for the GK SNF) and the Central Atlantic (for the GK WTVD). They are therefore the primary responsibility of Soviet naval forces, from which a majority would come from the Northern Fleet[d], and a portion, if they could transit the Danish Straits in time, from the Baltic Red Banner Fleet.

Both of these naval strategic support missions are vital to their respective GK 'customers'. Cutting the Central Atlantic SLOC could have a decisive effect on the outcome of a prolonged conventional war in Europe. NATO planning calls for some one and a half million men from the United States to reinforce Europe in the event of war. While most of them would be flown over, their equipment – about twelve million tons of goods – would have to be shipped over the Atlantic. In addition an estimated three thousand to six thousand shiploads (depending upon the types of ships which are available) per month of fuel, food, ammunition, spares, supplies and so forth would be required to keep the military, and the civilian, effort in Europe going.[31] Without this vital lifeline the NATO defences would soon wither. On the other hand the defence of the Arctic SSBN bastions is vital for the survival of the Soviet nuclear strategic reserves. There is a considerable danger that a sufficient number of Soviet SSNBs seeking to hide in Soviet northern home waters and

under the Arctic ice could be tracked and destroyed by NATO ASW SSNs, unless these SSNs could be prevented from reaching the SSBNs in the first place. This calls for concentrating Northern Fleet assets to the Norwegian Sea and North Atlantic, to establish an extended system of defence-in-depth against NATO SSNs. (See pages 33 to 35 for details)

However, it is vital to note that the Northern Fleet does not yet have the resources for conducting both campaigns at once. This places a strain on the resources of the Northern Fleet which is unlikely to have enough naval forces (mainly in the form of submarines and naval aviation) to effectively wage both campaigns simultaneously. Thus a choice will have to be made in the allocation of resources. In the opinion of this author it is almost certain that, at present force levels, the defence of the Arctic SSBN forces would receive priority. This is because these SSBNs constitute part of the Soviet main strategic nuclear forces and are of primary importance for the very survival of the Soviet Union, as well as constituting her only post-exchange nuclear bargaining force.[32] Thus it is likely that these forces have a far higher strategic planning priority than the conventional theatre operations in the Western TVD, and that therefore the use of naval assets for their defence will have priority over the use of the same naval assets for supporting the GK WTVD. It is also worth noting that this logic is supported by the rationale for the new United States 'Maritime Strategy' involving Forward Defence operations deliberately placing Soviet SSBNs in danger.[33] In addition a closer examination of Soviet submarine building programmes, and especially of their armament, appears to indicate a penchant towards long range ASW, and not, with the exception of the *Oscar* class SSGN, a major focus on long range anti-shipping. This does not mean that there would be a total lack of anti-SLOC operations in the Central Atlantic, but that the emphasis on this mission is, as things stand now, relatively small.

It is likely that the primary Soviet Northern Fleet wartime emphasis will be upon SSBN defence. This in turn would call for assistance from the IA PVO to provide air defence for the Soviet naval surface and air units seeking to prevent NATO ASW forces from penetrating the Norwegian Sea. This is dealt with in more detail in section 2.2.2, the important point here being that land based air support is vital if the Northern Fleet is to carry out its mission, and that effective air support requires airfields located closer to the Norwegian Sea and the GIFUK Gap than the present IA PVO Kola runways. In turn this calls for occupation and use of airfields in northern and western Fenno-scandia, preferably on the north Norwegian coastline. This in turn calls for ground operations in north-central Fenno-scandia to seize these areas, which bring us to the final, tertiary military campaign level in this area.

(d) NB: Henceforth the terms 'Northern Fleet' and 'Baltic Red Banner Fleet' will be used in their strict operational sense, ie as Operational level (in the Soviet sense – i.e. seventh in the ranking hierarchy) units containing only those forces capable of waging strictly naval operations on a front and army scale. Thus they are not used in the administrative sense, where the forces under the GK SNF also are included, as well as the amphibious forces.

Fenno-scandia and Soviet tertiary theatre support operations

The general scope of these tertiary frontlevel support operations for both the Northern Fleet command and the GK WTVD affecting Fenno-scandia is shown on Map 1.3. These consist respectively of:

For the GK WTVD: Securing his northern flank, which consists essentially of Denmark.

For the Commander Northern Fleet: Firstly neutralising enemy forces on, and probably securing, his south-eastern land flank, which consists of Northern Norway (NON). Secondly of neutralising enemy forces in the North Atlantic land littorals of Scotland, Iceland, Greenland's eastern coast, Jan Mayen and south Norway. Svalbard and Bear Island for their part would almost certainly be occupied within hours.

GK WTVD Front Operations affecting Fenno-scandia

In the first case, the occupation of the Danish straits is important for the GK WTVD so that he can cover his vulnerable northern flank. This is so for three main reasons. The first is related to the air war. The GK WTVD must ensure that NATO aircraft cannot use the Danish bases for deep strikes into the Soviet rear. Secondly, he must establish Soviet anti-aircraft defences in Denmark to prevent the transit of this area by NATO aircraft. Thirdly, he must assist the transit of Soviet aircraft through Danish airspace, and fourthly provide the use of Danish airfields as forward staging areas for deep strike/attack operations into the NATO rear areas, notably the United Kingdom and the Dutch and Belgian harbour complexes.

The second main reason why the Danish Straits must be occupied is related to the ground operations. Any Soviet offensive in Central Europe striking for the Rhine and beyond would be vulnerable to a massive encirclement operation unless its northern flank were secured. Here Jutland plays a key role, and especially the United States Marine Corps training for deployment to this area must be viewed with concern by Soviet planners. Should a large NATO amphibious assault take place here, followed by Allied heavy divisions disembarking directly here after the Atlantic crossing, it could threaten the Soviet spearhead located to the west in Central Europe. Therefore the GK WTVD must ensure that he controls the Jutland peninsula and can defend it against an Allied invasion.

Thirdly, it would be helpful to the GK WTVD if he could deny the use of the Baltic Straits to the Western naval forces. This can almost only be done by mining the Straits and occupying the adjacent land areas so as to defend the minefields. If this can be achieved the Soviet ASW mopping-up operations in the Baltic

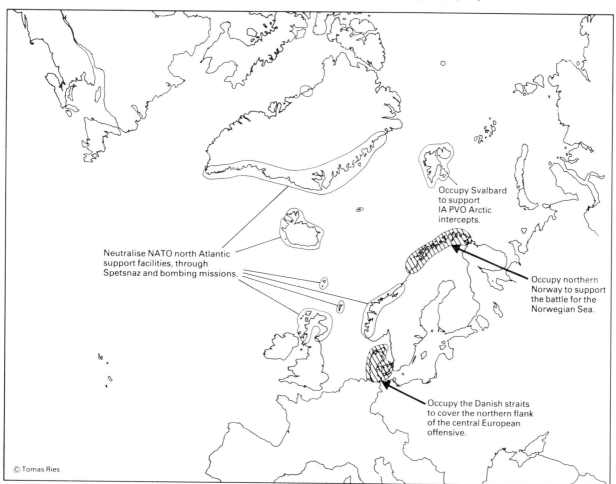

Occupy Svalbard to support IA PVO Arctic intercepts.

Neutralise NATO north Atlantic support facilities, through Spetsnaz and bombing missions.

Occupy northern Norway to support the battle for the Norwegian Sea.

Occupy the Danish straits to cover the northern flank of the central European offensive.

© Tomas Ries

MAP 1.3. Fenno-scandia and Soviet tertiary theatre support operations.

could permit the relatively safe use of Baltic SLOC for transporting vital Soviet logistic supplies to the fighting forces in Central Europe. This is vital as the Soviets must count very heavy destruction of their land transportation links by NATO, and without these supplies the fighting forces would be choked out. Secondly, occupation of the Straits might permit the Baltic Red Banner Fleet to exit her submarined forces into the North Sea, English Channel and the European maritime approaches, for anti-SLOC operations.

These are the main reasons for the front level operations against the Danish Straits. In order to accomplish this a combined ground and amphibious assault on the BALTAP command is necessary. This is the main responsibility of the Northern Front command, one of the four earmarked fronts under the GK WTVD. The Northern Front peacetime HQ is probably located at Fürstenburg in the northern DDR, and has as major subordinate commands: the 2nd Guards Tank Army, the East German V Military District forces (roughly the size of a Soviet Army Corps), the Air Corps North (roughly equivalent to one Frontal Aviation Army) and the combined Warsaw Pact (WAPA) amphibious force in the Baltic (consisting roughly of four brigades[e] in total) along with their transport fleet. This however only includes the main forces under the Northern Front command, and not the very numerous smaller specialised forces, such as WAPA Spetsnaz units, and so forth. Nor does it include the additional forces it could be allocated by the Stavka VGK should this be felt correct. These could include parachute division(s) from the Airborne Forces (K VDV), theatre bomber assistance from the Aviation Armies (K DA), and the entire Baltic Front, to mention but the main options.

It is important to note that the argument usually presented, that the Soviet Union would try to seize the Straits to permit the transit of surface and submarine vessels to and from the repair and replenishment wharves in the Baltic, is deliberately not included here. This author sees it as almost hopeless for the Soviet Union to envisage such use of the Straits in the face of their vulnerability to mining – both from the air and from submarine forces. However should the war become long, stretching over a period of months or more, then this use of the Straits could become important.

Front operations to support the Northern Fleet

For the Commander of the Northern Fleet front-level air, and probably ground and amphibious operations, in the north Atlantic coastal areas is a vital

support requirement. This is so for two main reasons. Firstly, he must prevent the use of these areas by NATO air and naval forces for strikes against his Kola basing infrastructure (only 450 kilometres from north Norwegian air bases). Secondly, he desperately needs land based air support for his own operations in the Norwegian Sea, and the bases on the Kola are too far removed to permit the type of sustained air cover which is required to be established. These operations, being directly related to the Kola, are outlined in more detail later in the text. The important point to note here is that to acquire these airbases the GK VPVO must have the support of the forces of the Arctic Detached Front. Which command therefore would have to engage in a front level operation to acquire and control forward airfields in northern Norway (NON) and possibly northern Sweden and northern Finland.

Note concerning the boundaries drawn on Map 1.4.

It is important to keep the following points in mind concerning the command and operational boundaries shown on Map 1.4.

1. These boundaries are tentative and based on the open sources indicated in note 34. It is quite possible that the line between the NW TVD and GK W TVD lies further south, along the northern border of Skåne in Sweden and encompassing all of southern Norway.

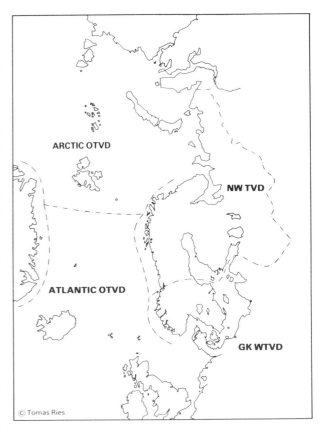

MAP 1.4. The Soviet TVD organisation of the Nordic Region

(e) NB: Brigade in the Soviet sense – i.e. a unit of about 3,000 men. Thus the Soviets dispose of a total of about 12,000 specially trained amphibious assault combat units in the Baltic.

This would depend very much upon the type of scenario one envisages. It is quite possible for the boundaries to be placed in different areas depending upon which overall wartime contingency the Soviet command applies. In other words, if a major emphasis is placed upon occupying northern Norway then the boundary might be drawn further south, to permit coordinated attacks on NATO bases in southern Norway and perhaps even a crossing through central Sweden. On the other hand if the major emphasis is placed upon occupying the Baltic Straits, then the boundary might be drawn further north, to permit operations against southern and central Norway and possibly through the same parts of Sweden, which in this case are integrated with the requirements of the Northern Front of the GK W TVD. Alternatively, in the case of an isolated attack against Sweden, it might encompass all of Sweden.

What appears quite certain however is that in the most likely wartime contingency, that of a general NATO-WAPA war, the Baltic Straits, the southern Baltic Sea, and probably southernmost Sweden, are part of the command area of the GK W TVD.

2. These command and operational boundaries are by no means static over time. They must be seen as flexible boundaries applying only to the opening stages of military operations. Once the campaign got underway they would no doubt be altered to suit the changing circumstances, priorities, and requirements of the main commands.

The result for the Nordic region

If we now look at what we call the 'Nordic region' it becomes clear that there is no such thing in Soviet military planning. Much as it may hurt Nordic egos, in

Soviet military operational terms there is no such entity as 'Northern Europe', or the 'Nordic region' or the 'Scandinavian states'. What does exist are two essentially distinct front level combat areas: the northern flank of the GK WTVD, consisting of the Baltic Straits, southern Sweden and possibly southern Norway; and the south-eastern coastal flank of the GK SNF north Atlantic theatre support operations, consisting of north-central Norway, Sweden and Finland. Thus Fenno-scandia is split in two, with the southern half of interest to the GK WTVD and the northern half of interest to the GK SNF and GK VPVO. The result is shown on Map 1.4, which shows the Nordic region as it is organised in Soviet military planning, including the Northern Front of the GK WTVD, the NW TVD, the Arctic OTVD and the Atlantic OTVD.[34]

SOVIET PRIMARY STRATEGIC, SECONDARY THEATRE, AND TERTIARY FRONTAL FORCES ADJACENT TO THE NORDIC REGION

We can now take a closer look at what general types of forces the Soviet military actually has deployed in the Nordic vicinity. By grouping these in their operational combat commands it is then possible to assess

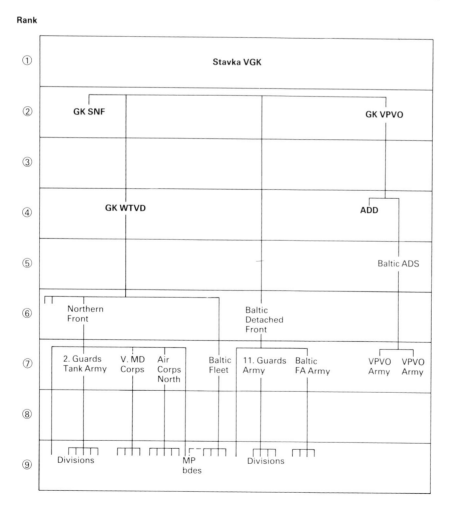

CHART 1.1 The Northern Front and the Baltic Detached Front as part of the overall Soviet Command Structure

their purpose, as well as their regional roles, in Soviet strategic planning.

Charts 1.1 (A) and 1.1.(B) outline the main Soviet combat commands down to the Operational-Tactical level which are active in the vicinity of the Nordic region. Chart 1.1.(A) shows the forces under the GK Western TVD adjacent to the Baltic, while Chart 1.1.(B) shows the commands in the North-western TVD.

These commands can be divided into three general types. The most important are those in the Strategic level (levels one to four). They represent primary Soviet strategic interests with a direct bearing on the survival of the Soviet Union. The next most important commands are those charged with major theatre-level operations in support of the strategic forces. They have an indirect relation to the survival of the Soviet Union in that the success or failure of their operations play a major part in determining the viability of the primary Strategic commands. These commands are probably not necessarily tied to a particular ranking level, the important criteria here being their relationship to the Stavka VGK. If this is direct (i.e. without

intermediate command links) it would appear to indicate a particular Stavka VGK concern with that particular commands missions which, though it strictly speaking does not merit a high command ranking in the military hierarchy, nonetheless is responsible for a vital task requiring direct monitoring. This would for instance be the case of the Operational Command of the Northern Fleet. The third and lowest command types included in this table are those charged with front level operations in support of the theatre level operations. The outcome of their missions has a bearing on the capacity of the theatre forces to achieve their objectives, and thus is one step further removed from primary Soviet vital interests.

From this perspective there are three types of forces. Primary strategic, with a direct bearing on Soviet security. Secondary strategic support forces charged with theatre-level operations with a direct bearing on the security of the strategic forces. And finally tertiary theatre support forces charged with front-level operations with a direct bearing on the capacity of the theatre forces to accomplish their missions. From this perspective the mission priority,

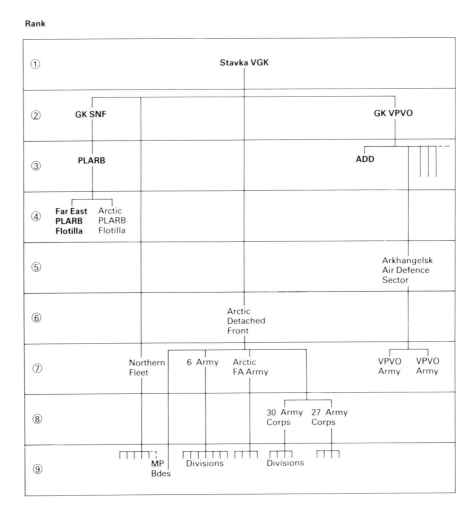

CHART 1.1 The Arctic PLARB Flotilla, the Arkhangelsk Air Defence Sector, the Arctic Detached Front and the Northern Fleet as part of the overall Soviet Command Structure

and command relationship, of the three types of forces in the region are also clear. Each of them shall now be briefly examined in turn.

Strategic forces next to Fenno-scandia

There are two major strategic commands with important elements of their forces based next to Fenno-scandia, and dependent upon the area to accomplish their main mission. These are the GK SNF with the PLARB Flotilla based on the Kola in the NW TVD, and the GK VPVO with the very important Arkhangelsk Air Defence Sector in the NW TVD and the Baltic Air Defence Sector in the northern part of the GK WTVD. Map 1.5 shows the main basing locations of these commands forces. It also includes the Forward Operating Locations (FOL) and dispersal airfields in this area of the 36 Aviation Army.

The forces of the GK SNF and GK VPVO strategic commands are, as noted earlier, responsible for the implementation of Soviet nuclear global strategy. The importance of the Kola Peninsula stems entirely from the fact that it happens to offer vital and in many cases unique basing and support facilities for important elements of both of these services. This is the primary reason for the strategic importance of the Kola area and the main impetus behind the Soviet build-up in the area. All other forces deployed to the area, such as the conventional forces of the Northern Fleet and the ground and tactical aviation forces of the Far Northern Independent Front, are purely secondary and on the whole a consequence of the Soviet global strategic nuclear requirements on the Kola. Their very existence in northern Fenno-scandia is indeed mainly a function of the extent to which they can provide secondary or tertiary support to the global nuclear strategy (through such support roles as Northern Fleet naval defence of the SSBN bases and Arctic concealment areas, and ground forces and frontal aviation forces assistance in this effort by occupying key stretches of the north Norwegian coastline). In the one case where they actually have an independent wartime military objective – the emerging Northern Fleet capability for denying the central Atlantic sea-lines-of-communication (SLOC) to NATO, which could have a decisive influence on the battle for Europe – its priority, from the overall strategic perspective, is still only secondary to that of struggling for security from a strategic nuclear attack. As such the Northern Fleet independent theatre mission of cutting central Atlantic SLOC exists only on sufferance that the primary responsibility – protecting the SSBN forces – is guaranteed.

Strategic support forces next to Fenno-scandia.

Map 1.6 shows the main basing areas of the regional strategic support forces deployed to the vicinity of Fenno-scandia. These consist of forces whose military operations decisively can influence either the security of the Strategic command's forces (for the PLARB of the GK SFN), or the outcome of the Strategic command's (for the GK WTVD). As noted earlier two such decisive theatre campaigns can be conducted by forces based next to the Nordic Region

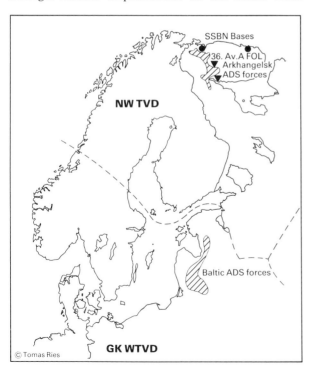

MAP 1.5. Soviet primary strategic forces in the Nordic Region

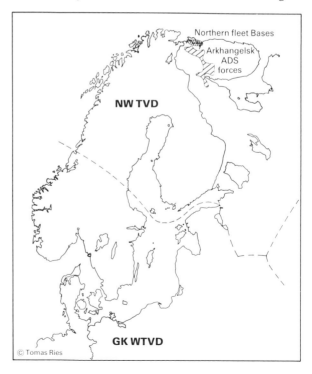

MAP 1.6. Soviet secondary theatre forces in the Nordic Region

and involving major military operations next to the Nordic Region. These are the theatre support mission for the GK SFN, involving the Northern Fleet defence-in-depth in the Norwegian Sea, and the theatre support mission for the GK WTVD, involving Northern Fleet sea-denial operations in the central Atlantic. As also noted earlier the Northern Fleet at present does not have the resources to conduct both campaigns simultaneously, and the emphasis will probably be upon defending the SSBNs.

This campaign essentially involves two combat commands:

Primarily the Northern Fleet, consisting of forces whose main task is the prosecution of naval combat for either sea control or sea denial. These consist of the main part of the Northern Fleet, excluding the amphibious assault vessels (which are under Northern Fleet executive command but probably are under the operational command of the Arctic Detached Front HQ).

Secondly, the Soviet strategic aerospace defence forces (Vojska PVO), however in this case tasked not with their primary strategic air defence mission against transmitting enemy strategic strike units, but with the theatre-level air support for the naval in-depth defence operations in the Norwegian Sea. Thus this IA PVO role will clearly be subordinate to the primary strategic requirements, and the availability of aircraft will therefore depend upon the strategic nuclear situation. In this case the allocated forces remain under Vojska PVO executive command, but are on request under the temporary operational control of the Stavka VGK, which, in consultation with the GK VPVO, can assign elements of the Arkhangelsk ADS IA PVO to assist the Northern Fleet.

It is ironic that it is the build-up in the northern waters of the first of these two services – namely the Soviet Northern Fleet – which has been most noted in the Western media and academic circles. This is probably because this is one of the more visible developments, and a relatively easily quantifiable subject. However, it is essential to note that this is only a small part of a far greater development, and that the Northern Fleet conventional forces are strictly a secondary military consideration in Soviet strategic planning. As such the growth of the Northern Fleet (in the operational sense of the term – ie not including the GK SNF SSBNs), despite its newsworthiness, is merely a symptom of underlying Soviet strategic interests and not a casual factor. This distinction is vital if one is to understand the nature of the Nordic strategic environment. However with the steady growth (in terms of the sum of quality plus quantity) of the Northern Fleet this may be changing slightly. Should the Soviet Union in the coming decade acquire the capability to establish a permanent naval presence in the Central Atlantic it is probable that the conventional elements of the Soviet Fleet may acquire a limited strategic value of their own for the Soviet leadership. This would partly be due to the increased wartime capability for cutting Central Atlantic SLOC which this would confer, and partly due also to the political consequences such a capability could have in Western Europe.

In this context it is also important to distinguish between peacetime, crisis and wartime use of military forces. In this study the Soviet military forces have been dealt with strictly from the perspective of their wartime organisation and use. However it is clear that military forces, particularly where naval forces are concerned, also can be exploited in peacetime as a means for acquiring political influence, applying pressure, etc. In this context the conventional forces of the Northern Fleet have a far greater role on the littoral states, such as Norway, than the strategic SSBNs or the Vojska PVO. And in this sense the study of the Northern Fleet *per se* is certainly justified, and, as noted, may become a strategic consideration in its own right in the years to come. Thus for a country like Norway a thorough and constantly updated analysis of the Northern Fleet is a vital task.

Theatre support forces next to Fennoscandia

Map 1.7 shows the deployment of theatre support forces to the Nordic Region. Unlike the previous two sections this includes important forces both in the GK WTVD sector and the NW TVD.

In the NW TVD their primary task is to support the operational requirements of the theatre-level VMF and Vojska PVO strategic support forces. To this end the Soviet military has deployed, and equally importantly developed the rapid reinforcement infrastructure for, a number of front level military forces in the Kola and adjacent regions. These forces, which may properly be considered as tertiary support forces, have their objectives entirely subordinated to the secondary theatre-level support requirements of the VMF and Vojska PVO.

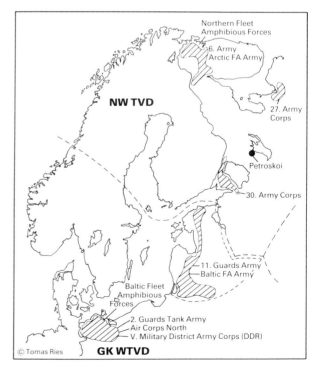

MAP 1.7. Soviet tertiary front forces in the Nordic Region

Since the Stavka VGK in this case is also in direct operational command of the Northern Fleet, of the Arkhangelsk ADS via the Vojska PVO High Command, and strategic/theatre bomber forces, it permits the integration of theatre and front level operations in northern Fenno-scandia, and the complete concentration of efforts here towards what is essentially, on the theatre-level, a strategic defensive operation, though probably involving considerable offensive operations on the Frontal level (such as occupation of key airfields in northern Norway, and certainly massed air strikes against airfields, naval bases, command centres, etc. throughout Norway).

This also provides another reason for the lack of a GK North-western TVD. Because the mission of the forces which would actually operate in the NW TVD (ie those subordinated to the Arctic Detached Front Command does not entail any strategic objectives *per se*, but are strictly to support the strategic forces in the far north, they can hardly be allocated a major Strategic level command. Such an integrated theatre headquarters, should it be established, would logically be an Atlantic OTVD High Command, since it is here that the main focus of the north-western military operations lies and since it is the outcome of the Battle for the Norwegian Sea which directly determines the security of the SSBNs, and not the battle for northern Norway. Although it is possible that such a GK Atlantic OTVD presently exists and is in charge of all theatre and front operations north-west of the GK WTVD, nobody has yet identified its leadership. Nor is it likely that the ground forces would readily agree to an operational command structure which placed their forces under a naval High Command, instead of vice versa. And considering the predominant position of the ground forces in the General Staff, such a factor could also play a major role.

As the General Staff is also in direct operational command of the Atlantic and Arctic OTVDs it permits the integration of military strategic support operations in the north-west which is vital since naval, theatre air defence and land operations in this area are intimately linked. In fact the distinguishing feature of the Far Northern Front area is that here – unlike in the Western TVD – land operations hold no strategic value *per se*, but are entirely a function of their contribution to the air and naval battles over and around Fenno-scandia. These in turn are characterised by their direct effect upon the security of the Soviet Strategic Nuclear Forces, and this is probably the rationale for why the Stavka VGK prefers to retain direct control of far northern operations rather than delegate them to an independent TVD HQ. There are other reasons as well, but as noted, this will not be dealt with here.

In the following sections of Part I the rationale for the deployment of these three basic types of forces to the Kola will be outlined in more detail. In addition, the relative strength of the deployment of these forces to the Kola, compared to the rest of the Soviet Union will be assessed, as one means of demonstrating the importance of the area in Soviet planning.

REFERENCES

1. A systematic empirical outline of these bases is provided in Part II.

2. See notably:

   SUVOROV, Viktor: *Inside the Soviet Army*. London, Hamish Hamilton, 1st. ed., 1982: pp. 296. (Especially Part I, Chapters 4–7, and Part II, Chapters 1–8: pp. 26–99)

   SUVOROV, Viktor: 'Strategic Command and Control. The Soviet approach.' *International Defense Review*, Vol. 17, No. 12, December 1984: pp. 1813–20.

   And indirectly:

   POLMAR, Norman: *Guide to the Soviet Navy*, Annapolis, Naval Institute Press, 3rd. ed., 1983: pp. 7–9. (In Chapter 4, 'Organisation and Command.')

   SCOTT, Harriet Fast and William F.: *The Armed Forces of the USSR*. London, Arms and Armour Press Ltd., 3rd. rev. ed., 1984: pp. 183–187. (Including Chart 16, 'Operational Structure of the Soviet Armed Forces.')

3. SCOTT, H. F. & W. F.: *The Armed . . .*, pp. 141–182.

4. SCOTT, H. F. & W. F.: *The Armed . . .*, pp. 141–144.

5. SUVOROV, V.: *Inside . . .*, p. 90.

6. SUVOROV, V.: *Inside . . .*, pp. 146, 153, 161, 166, 175.

7. SUVOROV, V.: p. 142.

8. SUVOROV, V.: *Inside . . .*, p. 90.

9. SUVOROV, V.: *Inside . . .*, p. 52.

10. SUVOROV, V.: *Inside . . .*, pp. 80, 84.

11. SCOTT, H. F. & W. F.: *The Armed . . .*, p. 189.

    SUVOROV, V.: 'Strategic Command . . .' p. 1815.

12. See:

    CUTSHAW, Charles Q.: 'Who's in Charge?' *United States Naval Institute Proceedings*, Vol. 112/4/998, April 1986: pp. 79–83.

    DEANE, Michael J., Ilana KASS and Andrew G. PORTH: 'The Soviet Command Structure in Transformation.' *Strategic Review*, Vol. XII, No. 2, spring 1984: pp. 55–70.

    HEMSLEY, Brigadier John: 'The Influence of Technology upon Soviet Operational Doctrine.' *RUSI Journal*, Vol. 131, No. 2, June 1986: pp. 21–28.

    HEMSLEY, John: 'Soviet Military Institutions.' *Soviet Troop Control*, London, Brasseys Defence Publishers Ltd., 1st ed., 1982: pp. 25–68.

    HINES, John G.: 'Soviet Front Operations in Europe. Planning for encirclement.' *Spotlight on the Soviet Union*, Report from a Conference at Sundsvollen, Report No. 1/86, Alumni Organisation of the Norwegian Defence College, Oslo, 1986: pp. 74–101.

HINES, John G. and Phillip A. PETERSEN: 'Is NATO Thinking too Small? A comparison of command structures.' *International Defense Review*, Vol. 19, No. 5, May 1986: pp. 563–578.

HINES, John G. and Phillip A. PETERSEN: 'Changing the Soviet System of Control. Focus on Theatre Warfare.' *International Defense Review*, Vol. 19, No. 3, March 1986: pp. 281–289.

HUTCHINSON, Robert: 'Wind of Change for the Soviet High Command.' *International Defense Review*, Vol. 15, No. 4, 1982: pp. 386–388.

PETERSEN, Phillip A.: 'Soviet Planning for Strategic Operations against NATO.' *Spotlight on the Soviet Union*, Report from a Conference at Sundsvollen, Report No. 1/86, Alumni Organisation of the Norwegian Defence College, Oslo, 1986: pp. 102–125.

URBAN, Mark: 'Organising the Juggernaut. Command, Control and Intelligence.' (Chapter 2) *Soviet Land Power*, London, Ian Allan Ltd., 1st ed., 1985: pp. 27–41.

SCOTT, William F.: 'Organisation of the Soviet Armed Forces.' *Air Force Magazine*, Vol. 69, No. 3, March 1986: pp. 62–74.

'Soviet Doctrine and Strategy.' *Soviet Military Power 1986*, Washington D. C., Dept. of Defense, 5th ed., March 1986: pp. 10–19.

SUVOROV, V.: 'Strategic Command . . .', pp. 1813–1820.

13. SUVOROV, V.: *Inside . . .*, pp. 37–38.

HINES, J. G. & P. A. PETERSEN: 'Changing . . .', pp. 185–188.

14. SUVOROV, V.: 'Strategic Command . . .', pp. 1817–1818.

15. SUVOROV, V.: 'Strategic Command . . .', pp. 1816–1820.

16. SUVOROV, V.: 'Strategic Command . . .', p. 1819.

HINES, J. G. & P. A. PETERSEN: 'Changing . . .', pp. 283–285.

17. SUVOROV, V.: 'Strategic Command . . .', p. 1814.

18. SUVOROV, V.: 'Strategic Command . . .', p. 1817.

HINES, J. G. & P. A. PETERSEN: 'Changing . . .', p. 288.

19. SUVOROV, V.: 'Strategic Command . . .', p. 1815.

20. HINES, J. G. & P.A. PETERSEN: 'Is NATO thinking . . .', p. 564.

POLMAR, Norman: *Guide to the Soviet Navy*. Annapolis, Naval Institute Press, 3rd. rev. ed., 1983: p. 7.

SCOTT, H. F. & W. F.: *The Armed . . .*, pp. 106, 111, 115, 122.

SUVOROV, V.: 'Strategic Command . . .', pp. 1815, 1816, 1820.

SUVOROV, V.: *Inside . . .*, p. 37.

21. See notably SUVOROV, V.: 'Strategic Command . . .', p. 1820, for an outline of the relationship of Soviet high commands and their level in Soviet Military Art.

22. SUVOROV, V.: 'Strategic Command . . .', p. 1815.

23. Cited in: SCOTT, H. F. & W. F.: *The Armed . . .*, p. 150.

24. SCOTT, William F.: 'The Soviets and Strategic Defense.' *Air Force Magazine*, Vol. 69, No. 3, March 1986: pp. 41–45.

25. SCOTT, H. F. and W. F.: *The Armed . . .*, pp. 159–160.

26. SUVOROV, V.: 'Strategic Command . . .', p. 1820.

27. SUVOROV, V.: 'Strategic Command . . .', p. 1820.

28. SUVOROV, V.: 'Strategic Command . . .', p. 1820.

29. SUVOROV, V.: 'Strategic Command . . .', p. 1820.

It is worth noting that there are also indications that Soviet Army Corps are on the same command level as full Armies. In this case both would be Operational level formations, though the Army Corps would command less resources – ie incorporate less artillery support, etc.

30. SUVOROV, V.: 'Strategic Command . . .', p. 1820.

31. SWARZTRAUBER, Rear Admiral Sayre A.: 'The Potential Battle of the Atlantic,' *United States Naval Institute Proceedings*, Vol. 105/5/915, May 1979: p. 113.

32. For an excellent treatment of the evolution and present role of the Soviet SSBN force see notably: MccGwire, Michael: 'The Rationale for the Development of Soviet Seapower.' *United States Naval Institute Proceedings*, Vol. 106, No. 5, May 1980: pp. 155–183.

While six years old this paper provides a very thoughtful analysis of the role and importance of the Soviet SSBN forces, the essence of which, though the US SDI programme has added potential future missions to the Soviet SSBNs, still holds true today.

33. See: WATKINS, CNO Admiral James D.: 'The Maritime Strategy.' *United States Naval Institute Proceedings*, Vol. 112/1/995, January 1986: pp. 2–17.

34. See for instance:

AUSLAND, John C.: 'Ny sovjetstrategi i Europa?' *Forsvarets Forum*, No. 4, 1984: p. 5.

URBAN, M.: *Soviet Land Power*. London, Ian Allan Ltd., 1st. ed., 1985: p. 36.

CHAPTER 2

The Relative Deployment of Soviet Forces in the Kola

Now that we have outlined what the Soviet military forces deployed to the Kola actually consist of and what they represent, it is time to examine why they have been placed there. This is important because it provides us with an understanding of the underlying reasons for the evolution of the Nordic strategic environment. In addition the relative deployment of these military forces to the Kola, compared to deployments to other parts of the Soviet Union, is analysed. The purpose of this is to provide an idea of the relative importance of the Kola and adjacent areas to Soviet grand strategy.

STRATEGIC FORCES ON THE KOLA.

The strategic forces on the Kola Peninsula give the area strategic importance and focus both Soviet and US interests on this far northern region. These forces, being extra-regionally oriented and part of the central strategic nuclear balance between the Soviet Union and primarily the United States of America do not directly affect the regional Nordic military situation, but they do form the basic driving force underlying superpower military interest in northern Fennoscandia.

As noted earlier there are two main types of Soviet strategic nuclear forces operating from the Kola: the strategic offensive arm, and the strategic defensive arm. Each of these will be dealt with in turn below.

Soviet intercontinental nuclear forces on the Kola.

The Soviet strategic nuclear offensive arm includes three main services.

The ICBM Forces.
RVSN (*Raketnyye Voyska Strategicheskovo Naznacheniya*)

The Intercontinental SLBM Forces.
PLARB (*Podvodnaya Lodka Atombaya Raketnaya Ballisticheskaya*)[1]
The Intercontinental Long Range Aviation.
DA (*Dal'nyaya Aviatsiya*)[2]

As mentioned above the strategic SLBM forces and the intercontinental range elements of the Long Range Aviation are only part of the Navy and Air Force for administrative purposes, and the C-in-Cs of these two services exercise no direct operational control over them at all. For this they are under the direct combined operational control, in peacetime as well as in wartime, of the GK SNF under the Stavka VGK. In this respect they should be seen as a single service, and it is a fallacy to consider that the Soviet SSBN forces with intercontinental range SLBMs are part of the Soviet Fleet. They are so only insofar as the VMF is responsible for their development and upkeep, much like a Military District HQ is responsible for the peacetime administration of military forces in its area, but has absolutely no operational command over the forces in its district and no wartime command role beyond logistics. Thus the 'Northern Fleet' for instance is not in operational command of the SSBNs based in its area, though it probably is in executive command of these ships. Its main function in this respect is to maintain the SSBNs at the disposal of the Strategic Nuclear Forces section of the Stavka VGK, which is the actual operational command authority. Exactly the same logic applies to the DA.

These strategic nuclear forces are probably the single most important service in Soviet strategic planning, and a vital element in the Soviet perception of her own security requirements. It follows that any area in which the strategic operational units are deployed is of central importance to Soviet strategic security. As a consequence any such area will receive a high priority in Soviet military planning.

Of the three forces listed as part of the Strategic Nuclear Forces of the Soviet Union the Kola peninsula is of operational importance for the second (two PLARB Flotillas) and third (36 Aviation Army). The main branch, the Strategic Rocket Forces, is mainly based in a long belt across the central Soviet Union and for their operation and security the Kola is relatively unimportant. However the latter two services are both quite dependent upon the Kola, and do represent a considerable portion of the total Soviet nuclear strategic strike force. Table 2.1 shows the relative strengths of the three branches of the strategic nuclear offensive arm, in terms of their relative number of launch platforms (ICBMs, SLBMs and intercontinental range bombers), their relative number of warheads and, which in Soviet planning is seen as particularly important, in terms of the equivalent megatonnage (EMT) each service possesses. Unlike the United States strategic nuclear offensive forces (see next section) the proportional relationship of the three services in each of these three scales is the same, with the Strategic Rocket Forces having most launch platforms, warheads and EMT, the SLBM forces coming in second place, and the long range bomber force in third.

From this perspective the relative importance of the three services appears to be, in order of importance, the following:

> ICBM forces.
> Intercontinental range SLBM forces.
> Intercontinental range bomber forces.

While this ranking probably is accurate today it must be qualified by two key considerations, each of which increase the relative importance of the strategic submarine and bomber forces.

Firstly, as has been argued by Michael MccGwire[3],

TABLE 2.1. The Relative Strength of Soviet Intercontinental Nuclear Forces, 1985.

A.   **Total Numbers.**

Type	Launch Platforms	Warheads	EMT
ICBM	1,398	6,420	4,165
SLBM	979	2,787+	1,158
LRB	170	680	514
Total:	2,547	9,987	5,837

B.   **Percentage of Total Force.**

Type	Launch Platforms	Warheads	EMT
ICBM	54.9%	64.3%	71.4%
SLBM	38.4%	28.9%	19.8%
LRB	6.7%	6.8%	8.8%

Source: *The Military Balance 1985–1986.* pp. 180–181.

the Soviet SLBM forces occupy a special and unique place in Soviet nuclear strategy as the only force which – because of its capability for underwater concealment – can be retained as a strategic nuclear reserve for post-exchange use or bargaining purposes. Thus, despite its quantitatively second position in the triad, it probably occupies a very special and important place for Soviet strategic planners.

Secondly, though the Soviet long range bomber force ever since the mid 60s has held a very minor place in the Soviet strategic nuclear arsenal, this could be changing at present. The symptoms of the change are evident in the deployment of the *Bear* H bomber and the AS-15 ALCM, as well as in the production of the *Blackjack* intercontinental bomber. All three of these systems will considerably boost the potency of this force, which has not received any important new equipment for over two decades now. The rationale for the coming importance of the strategic bomber force on the other hand is two-fold. Firstly, as the United States strategic ASW and ICBM targeting capabilities increase – from the Soviet perception – the vulnerability of Soviet ICBMs and SSBNs, the importance of boosting the capabilities of the DA increases. Secondly, with the development of the US SDI programme there is the danger of a significant number of trans-atmospheric ICBMs and SLBMs being neutralised. Should such a situation arise – and the Soviet strategic planners have to take this possibility under serious consideration – the importance of low-trajectory/endoatmospheric strategic nuclear systems, such as intercontinental bombers and short/medium range SLBMs fired from the vicinity of the United States coasts, will increase considerably.

Thus the importance of the second and third services of the strategic nuclear offensive force is and will be greater than the quantitative analysis alone indicates. Both of these forces have important detachments dependent upon the Kola. To understand why this is so the basing and operational requirements of each of them will briefly be outlined.

The Kola and Soviet intercontinental SLBM forces.

The Soviet SSBN forces armed with intercontinental range SLBMs are the second most important strategic nuclear asset in the Soviet armed forces, and are the only strategic nuclear reserve force of the Soviet Union. As noted earlier they are only nominally part of the Soviet Navy, insofar as the VMF is responsible for their upkeep, but are operationally part of the strategic nuclear forces, under the direct operational command of the General Staff acting for the Stavka VGK.

Map 2.1 shows the two main basing areas where Soviet SSBNs armed with intercontinental range SLBMs are deployed, as well as their main oceanic

MAP 2.1. Soviet strategic SSBN basing and operating areas.

TABLE 2.2.(A) The Relative Deployment of Soviet Strategic Submarines with Intercontinental Range Ballistic Missles, 1985.

Total Numbers.

Type	Submarines Kola/Total	SLBM Kola/Total	Warheads Kola/Total	EMT Kola/Total
DELTA IV	1/1	16/16	n.a./n.a.	n.a./n.a.
TYPHOON	4/4	80/80	720/720	200/200
DELTA III	10/14	160/224	1,120/1,568	335/470
YANKEE II	1/1	12/12	12/12	12/12
DELTA II	4/4	64/64	64/64	56/56
DELTA I	10/18	120/216	120/216	104/186
HOTEL III	1/1	6/6	6/6	5/5
GOLF III	1/1	6/6	6/6	5/5
YANKEE I	10/19	160/304	160/304	102/180
Total:	42/63	624/928	2,208/2,896	819/1,114

Source: *The Military Balance 1985–1986*. pp. 21, 180–181.

TABLE 2.2.(B) Relative Deployment to the Kola Peninsula of Soviet Strategic Submarines with Intercontinental Range Ballistic Missiles, 1985.

Relative Distribution.

Type	Submarines Kola/Total	SLBM Kola/Total	Warheads Kola/Total	EMT Kola/Total
DELTA IV	100%	100%	100%	100%
TYPHOON	100%	100%	100%	100%
DELTA III	71%	71%	71%	71%
YANKEE II	100%	100%	100%	100%
DELTA II	100%	100%	100%	100%
DELTA I	55%	55%	55%	55%
HOTEL III	100%	100%	100%	100%
GOLF III	100%	100%	100%	100%
YANKEE I	57%	57%	57%	57%
Total:	66%	67%	76%	73%
Total post 80:	100%	100%	100%	100%

Source: *The Military Balance 1985–1986*. pp. 21, 180–181.

concealment areas. Of the two basing areas marked, the Kola is by far the most important area both in terms of absolute numbers but also in terms of priority of modern equipment.

This is indicated in Tables 2.2.(A) and (B) which show the detailed basing distribution of Soviet SSBNs carrying intercontinental range SLBMs in 1985. From this it is apparent that 66 per cent of the total force is based on the Kola Peninsula, and one hundred per cent of the most modern SSBNs, consisting of the *Typhoon* and *Delta* IV classes. As a result the actual relative importance of the Kola as a basing area for Soviet SSBN forces has increased considerably in the last five years, as each of these new submarines carries SLBMs with nine and seven warheads each respectively, as opposed to the single and three warheads of the earlier SLBM's. Thus, when measured in terms of warheads and EMT the actual importance of the Kola has grown to seventy-six per cent of the total SLBM warhead arsenal and seventy-three per cent of the EMT total.

This is mainly due to two factors:

The relatively advantageous defensive position of the Kola from naval and airborne attack.

The proximity, and suitable transit possibilities, of the Kola to the Arctic waters.

In the first case the situation is exactly the opposite to earlier requirements. Before the advent of the inter-continental range SLBMs a major Soviet naval basing consideration was access to the US Atlantic and Pacific coastal launch areas. However, since the early 70s, when the deployment of intercontinental range SS-N-8 mod 1 SLBMs permitted Soviet SSBNs to target all continental United States targets from rela-tively protected Soviet coastal waters, exactly the opposite consideration became important, with a Soviet priority on basing SSBNs in those areas which offered the maximum geographical defensive advan-tage to the Soviet Union against potential Western ASW forces. Two areas offer such possibilities: the Sea of Okhotsk, where the secondary Soviet SSBN base at Talinskaia Bay in Petropavlovsk is situated, and the Arctic waters off the Kola, where the main Soviet SSBN bases have been sited. Both of these areas provide the maximum opportunities for the

Soviet efforts to screen off their SSBN underwater hiding areas from western surface and air ASW forces.

However, as of the late 1970s this was no longer enough. At this point it became clear that United States' submarine based ASW capabilities had increased to the point where the Soviet capability to deny SSBN operating waters to Western surface and air forces no longer was sufficient. From this point on it became necessary to shield the SSBNs from the Western SSN forces. For this, deployment to restricted coastal waters was also no longer sufficient, as the various incidents involved in 'Operation Holystone' indicate. These involved the undetected operation of USN SSNs in the immediate vicinity of the Soviet SSBN bases and even within their harbour areas.[4] Their task was part of a very large scale USN integrated submarine tracking programme, involving satellite and aerial reconnaissance of Soviet submarine bases, detecting departing and returning Soviet submarines, USN spy submarines and other underwater detection systems next to the bases recording the accoustic signatures of departing and returning Soviet submarines, plus further Western submarines on station off the bases to follow key Soviet submarines, including SSBNs. This project also involved further naval forces beyond the Soviet protected inner sea and air space, such as the GIFUK and Aleutian SOSUS chains, and naval surface and air units tracking selected Soviet submarines. However, for the security of the Soviet strategic SSBNs it was the operations in her protected inner waters which were of most concern, as they indicated that a considerable threat to the Soviet SSBN forces existed, and that the VMF, with prevailing Soviet technology, could not deal with it. In fact it appears that USN and RN SSNs can operate virtually undetected in the most highly protected Soviet waters. These missions have only been officially mentioned when the USN submarines have has minor collisions with Soviet submarines, as had happened in Vladivostock harbour, in the mouth of the White Sea and on other occasions.[5] In each case the Soviets appear to have been ignorant of the presence of the USN SSNs, and unable, after the collision, to track the departing Western submarines.

For the VMF the message is clearly that deployment of the SSBNs to waters where the surface and airspace can be secured is not enough. They also have to go someplace where the sophisticated Western ASW technology will have trouble tracking them. Such an area appears to exist in the Arctic under-ice waters, and it is significant that all the most modern Soviet SSBNs appear to be specially constructed for under-ice operations.

For the strategic environment of the Nordic states this development is vital as the only existing Soviet basing area with suitable access to the Arctic under-ice areas is the Kola Peninsula. Map 2.1 shows the main Arctic operating areas of Soviet SSBNs and the very limited access and egress routes to the Arctic Ocean with the Kola as one of the optimal existing basing locations. This means that, until the time when the Soviet Union has constructed a new SSBN base somewhere along her Arctic coast, the Kola will be the most secure basing area for the most modern Soviet SSBNs. And it is worth noting that a single *Typhoon* equals more than eleven *Delta* III class SSBNs in terms of numbers of warheads carried. They are also more reliable, accurate and secure than earlier missiles, and in this sense also means that the Kola grows in importance for Soviet strategic planners.

The Kola and Soviet intercontinental bomber forces.

The Soviet intercontinental strategic nuclear bomber force is the third most important element in the Soviet strategic nuclear arsenal, and as noted earlier, both its quantitative importance and its strategic value to the Soviet Union is presently growing.

The actual strategic aviation forces themselves are divided into five Air Armies, of which only one is actually relevant to the Soviet intercontinental nuclear strike capability. These are:[6]

46 Air Army	HQ Smolensk, Byelorussia.	7 regiments Tu-16 3 regiments Tu-22 2 regiments Tu-26
24 Air Army	HQ Legnica, Poland.	5 regiments Su-24
4 Air Army	HQ Venitza, Ukraine.	5 regiments Su-24
30 Air Army	HQ Irkutsk, Siberia.	2 regiments Tu-16 3 regiments Su-24 2 regiments Tu-26
36 Air Army	HQ Moscow.	2 divisions M-4 2 divisions Tu-95

These strategic aviation forces consist of two main types of operational units. On the one hand these include the medium range bombers, including the Tu-16 *Badger*, Tu-22 *Blinder*, Tu-26 *Backfire*, and Su-24 *Fencer*. These forces are primarily for theatre support operations, and are allocated to four of the five Air Armies. These are: the 46 Air Army, which is the European Strategic Strike Force with 'swing' assets capable of being directed by the Stavka VGK against any area in the Western Strategic Direction at very short notice; the 24 Air Army and 4 Air Army, both of which are European Theatre Strike Forces, capable of being directed by the Stavka VGK against any targets in the Western TVD and Far Northern Front and the South-western and Southern TVDs respectively at short notice; and the 30 Air Army, which is the Far Eastern Strategic Strike Force, capable of being directed by the Stavka VGK against targets in the Far East at short notice. Of course all of these forces could be redirected to other directions given the time, but their characteristic feature is that they do not possess the range for intercontinental strategic nuclear bombing missions, and in this sense do not play a major role in the central strategic nuclear balance *vis-à-vis* the United States of America.[7]

This last mission is in the hands of the 36 Air Army with its HQ in Moscow and four main European bases plus one in the Far East. This Army is equipped with intercontinental range nuclear bombers, and is relevant for the central strategic nuclear balance.

The Kola Peninsula is important for this force by virtue of its location beneath the shortest flight path from the concentration of the 36 Air Army main bases to strategic targets in the United States. Map 2.2 shows the peacetime main bases of the 36 Air Army, the main Arctic dispersal and forward operating locations (FOL), and the shortest flight paths to their North American targets.[8] From this it is clear that a majority of the main bases lie between the Kola and the United States. Nonetheless, in time of crisis or war it is likely that the General Staff would seek to disperse the bombers to a maximum or secondary FOL, shown on the map along the Arctic coast. Thus only a smaller portion of the bombers would probably – and again the figures would vary depending upon the scenario – require the Kola facilities. Table 2.3 gives a general quantitative breakdown of the intercontinental bomber support assets located on the Kola. Again it is worth noting that these figures are likely to vary very widely depending upon the scenario, but the table serves to give a rough indication of the role the Kola plays for this portion of the force. More accurate data about actual bases is provided in Part II.

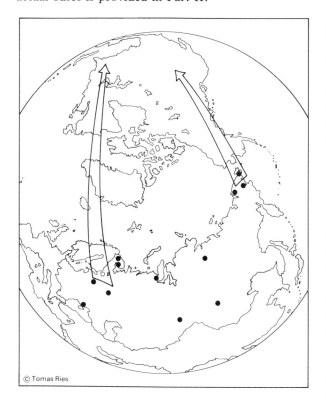

MAP 2.2. 36 Aviation Army Main Peacetime Bases, FOL, and main transit routes to key United States target areas.

TABLE 2.3 The Relative Importance of the Kola Peninsula for the Soviet Long-Range Strategic Bomber Force, 1985.

Type of Installation	Total USSR	Total Kola	Percentage Kola
Peacetime Main Bases	5	0	0%
Wartime Main Dispersal Bases	6 (+1)	1 (+1)	16% (28%)
Percentage Main Bases South of Kola (1)			80%

(1) For the intercontinental range portion of the strategic aviation armies of the Soviet Union.

Source: *Militaerbalansen 1984–1985.* pp. 29, 98.

Summary of the role of the Kola area for the Soviet strategic offensive forces.

With sixty-six per cent of the Soviet SSBN forces based on the Kola, and roughly thirty per cent of the intercontinental strategic bombers dependent upon Kola and adjacent forward operating locations, the Kola area is vital for the operations of roughly:

27.3 per cent of the total Soviet arsenal of strategic intercontinental launch platforms.

21 per cent of the total Soviet strategic intercontinental warhead inventory.

15.6 per cent of the total Soviet strategic intercontinentally deliverable EMT.

Clearly these figures are very rough and subject to a number of variations, but they do serve to provide a general indication of the relative importance of the Kola in overall Soviet nuclear strategy. In addition it is important to note that, as mentioned earlier, the Kola also is the most important base for the only Soviet strategic nuclear reserve force, in the form of the SSBNs. As such the Kola's strategic importance is far greater than that indicated merely by any quantitative analysis of numbers of deployed forces.

The GK VPVO and the Kola.

In addition to the role the Kola plays in Soviet offensive nuclear strategy, its importance in overall Soviet strategy is compounded by the contribution it makes to Soviet strategic defensive efforts. These are mainly the responsibility of the Soviet strategic aerospace command (Vojska PVO) with, to some extent, elements of the conventional forces of the Soviet Navy in certain circumstances performing a strategic defensive role by countering Western SSBN and SSGN forces. However one should note that this task has probably diminished considerably since the early 70s, when it became clear that the deployment of the Trident combined with Soviet technical difficulties with ASW technology made this a virtually hopeless task.

An important portion of the total Soviet strategic air

and naval defence assets are based on the Kola indicating its role also in this sense. However before examining these forces it is necessary to understand why the Kola is, in the strategic defensive sense, importantly located for the Soviet Union. To do this it is useful to take a close look at the threat.

The Strategic Nuclear Threat to the Soviet Union.

The strategic nuclear threat to the Soviet Union is composed of six primary elements. These are:

> ICBMs.
> Intercontinental range SLBMs.
> Intercontinental range bombers.
> Medium range ground launched nuclear missiles.
> Medium range sea launched nuclear missiles.
> Medium range nuclear capable aircraft.

The strategic importance of any area for defence against these threats is a function of two main factors. Firstly, whether the area is located under or near to the likely transit route of the potential attacking forces. This is important as it is a major determinant of the suitability of that area for locating incoming enemy forces for early warning of an attack, for tracking, for target acquisition, and for interception, whether it be by ABM defence systems (laser and missiles), aircraft or SAM systems. Secondly, whether the area is located near to the potential launch site of enemy nuclear forces. This is important both in regard to intercontinental systems, as it determines the stage at which you are able to acquire direct 'line of sight' radar acquisition of incoming forces, which remains important for target acquistion and computing flight paths, and with regard to shorter range attacking forces, as it determines whether the location provides basing facilities for forces which could carry out a pre-emptive strike on the enemy launch platform. This could involve either air attacks against potentially threatening airfields or ground based missile sites, or naval operations against threatening submarines carrying either shorter range SLBMs, or SLCMs.

From this perspective the Kola Peninsula is, for geographical reasons, mainly of strategic defensive importance to the Soviet Union in relation to the US ICBM threat, the US intercontinental range bomber threat and the medium range sea launched nuclear missile threat. This is clearly only a portion of the total threat. Table 2.4.(A) outlines the whole range of the strategic nuclear threat to the Soviet Union. This includes, in addition to US intercontinental forces, the following:

What the Soviet Union calls 'Forward Based Systems', including United States Army Pershing II and GLCM missiles stationed in Western Europe and USAF and USN nuclear capable aircraft which could launch nuclear strike missions against the Soviet heartland west of the Urals from airfields in Western Europe.

The strategic nuclear threat presented by Chinese, French and British nuclear forces, including both ICBMs, intercontinental and medium range SLBMs and medium and short range nuclear capable aircraft.

TABLE 2.4.(A) The Relative Launcher Strength of United States, United Kingdom, French and PRC Intercontinental Nuclear Forces, 1985.

Type	US	UK	Fr	PRC
ICBM/IRBM	1,130	–	18	6
SLBM	616	64	80	12
LRB/MRB	ca 700	123	51	120
Total:	1,814	187	149	138

NB: The ICBM/IRBM figures include those missiles which can reach the Soviet heartland west of the Urals. Thus the 60 DF-3 IRBM in the PRC (range 2,700 kilometres) are not included. On the other hand the United States figure does include the GLCM and Pershing II's stationed in Europe.

The same applies to the SLBM figures, which excludes the 12 HY-2 SLBM in the PRC (range 2,200–3,000 kilometres).

The LRB/MRB figures include for the United States Strategic Air Command's strategic bomber forces plus the nuclear capable aircraft forming part of United States Air Forces Europe (USAFE). The French figures include the Mirage IVA and IIIE, while the British represent the Tornado IDS.

Source: *The Military Balance 1985–1986.* pp. 158–161.

All of these forces tend to decrease the strategic importance of the Kola as, in most cases, their launch areas and/or flight routes do not affect that area. Map 2.3.(A) shows their main basing areas and direct transit routes to the Soviet strategic heartland, demonstrating the relatively peripheral role of the Kola from this perspective.

However, as the table indicates, it is the United States nuclear arsenal which presents the main strategic nuclear threat to the Soviet Union. In addition the

MAP 2.3.(A) The nuclear threat to the Soviet Union from the United Kingdom, France and China.

United States of America appears to be considered by Soviet strategic planners as the main adversary. And when it comes to the strategic nuclear threat it is those forces which are part of the United States Single Integrated Operations Plan (SIOP)[9], mainly the forces included in the so called nuclear triad – ICBMs, SLBMs and intercontinental bombers – which present the main strategic threat. It is thus understandable that Soviet strategic defensive systems have been concentrated towards countering this threat.

Map 2.3.(B) shows the main launch and transit routes of US SIOP allocated forces, minus the SSBNs. Equipped with the Trident this last force is able to target the Soviet Union from such a variety of oceans that it is useless to seek to mark them on this map. However it is almost certain that they would be launched from areas far away from the Norwegian Sea. One should note in passing that the Soviet strategic heartland, both in counterforce and countervalue terms, still lies west of the Urals, despite a shift of industrial and military (mainly the advent of the ICBMs) assets eastwards over the last thirty years. While it is clear that actual transit routes would vary very much, the map does give a rough idea of the value of the Kola from a strategic aerospace perspective, and does indicate that both for detection and interception efforts against ICBMs and strategic bombers the Kola is situated in a key location.

Table 2.4.(B) shows the relative strength of the United States intercontinental nuclear forces. Here a very interesting fact emerges. While the ICBMs

TABLE 2.4.(B) The Relative Strength of United States Intercontinental Nuclear Forces, 1985.

A.	Total Numbers.		
Type	Launch Platforms	Warheads	EMT
ICBM	1,018	2,118	1,279
SLBM	616	5,536	951
LRB	180	2,520	1,395
Total:	1,814	10,175	3,635

B.	Percentage of Total Force.		
Type	Launch Platforms	Warheads	EMT
ICBM	56.2%	20.8%	35.3%
SLBM	33.9%	54.4%	26.2%
LRB	9.9%	24.8%	38.5%

Source: *The Military Balance 1985–1986.* pp. 180–181.

account for most launch platforms, and the bombers for the least, the bombers, in terms of EMT, represent by far the most severe threat to the Soviet Union. This is due to a variety of factors, but what it does account for is the considerable emphasis the Soviet Union has placed on the strategic fighter interceptor forces (IA PVO) of the Vojska PVO. It also considerably enhances the importance of the Kola. With the deployment of the B-1B and ALCM, and judging by the apparently very large scale emphasis upon developing the 'stealth' bomber force, the strategic importance of the United States bomber force is likely to grow in the years to come.

Finally, one should add the relatively small threat posed by those Western SSBNs and SSGNs with launch areas in the Norwegian Sea, North Sea and north of here. These consist partly of the declining strategic threat from the ageing French M-1, M-2 and M-20 SLBMs (max. range 3,000 kilometres), presently being replaced by the M-4 (4,400+), and partly from the growing theatre threat posed by the growing deployment of the BGM-109A Tomahawk SLCM (max. range 2,500 kilometres) to United States Navy *Los Angeles* class SSN. In the first case the potential for Soviet strategic ASW attempts in the Norwegian Sea is declining, as the longer range of the M-4 permits deployment south of the GIFUK gap. In the second case on the other hand the incentives for increasing the strategic ASW capacities of the Northern Fleet are growing, even if, from a broader strategic perspective, the threat from the United States SLCM is only very small when compared to that from the SIOP allocated triad forces.

As a result the Kola is strategically located in relation to the flight paths of United States ICBMs and strategic nuclear bombers, and is suitably located for Soviet pre-launch neutralisation efforts of a

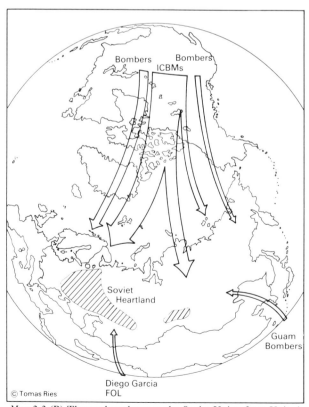

MAP 2.3.(B) The nuclear threat to the Soviet Union from United States SIOP allocated forces, excluding SSBNs.

portion of Western medium range SLBMs and SLCMs. The United States ICBM and LRB threat alone represents some 45.6 per cent of the total United States SIOP warhead threat against the Soviet Union and 73.8 per cent of the total United States SIOP EMT threat. With the large majority of Soviet targets strategic countervalue and counterforce targets remaining south of the Kola this means that a significant proportion of United States' SIOP forces would, in the event of a strike, pass over the Kola. This is why this area has a relatively high priority in Soviet aerospace effort.

The GK VPVO and the Kola.

As a result of this general threat picture the Soviet Union has deployed a certain number of Vojska PVO forces to the Kola. However before outlining these it is useful briefly to outline the main components of the Vojska PVO. These consist of five main services.[10]

Fighter Aviation of the Air Defence.
IA PVO (Istrebitel'naja Aviatsija PVO)

Zenith Rocket Troops.
ZRV (Zenitnyye Raketnyye Vojska)

Radio Technical Troops.
RTV (Radiotekhnichesiye Vojska)

Antispace Defence.
PRO (Protivoraketnaja Oborona)

The IA PVO comprises all the fighter interceptor assets of the Vojska PVO. These total over 1,200. In addition, following the reorganisation of the Soviet Air Forces between 1979 and 1985 the IA PVO disposes of an additional 2,800 mainly shorter range interceptors from the former FA commands. The main task of the IA PVO is, in conjunction with the RTV, the interception of enemy strategic bombers and the interception of enemy theatre bombers. In addition, under certain circumstances, the General Staff may allocate portions of the IA PVO to TVD commanders. These forces would remain under the executive command of the regional IA PVO commander, but would be under the operational command, for that specific operation, of the TVD or Independent Front command.

The ZRV comprises all the strategic SAM systems excluding those with an ABM capability (*Galosh* and *Gazelle*). These total over 1,200 SAM launch complexes, each with up to a dozen actual launch sites. In addition, following the reorganisation of the Soviet Armed Forces 1979–1985, the ZRV has been given operational command of the Troops of Air Defence of the Ground Forces (PVO SV) with front and tactical SAM and AAA assets. The main task of the ZRV is the strategic long range SAM interception of transiting enemy strategic bombers and point defence of strategic targets. In addition it is responsible for the theatre air defence on the operational and tactical levels of key theatre assets and operations.

The RTV consists of the strategic air defence radar networks, and is responsible for operation of all radar systems and providing targeting data to the IA PVO and ZRV. As such it also operates the AEW and AWACS aircraft of the Vojska PVO. The RTV probably also includes the EW radars (*Hen House*, phased array, OTH) and the early warning satellite system, even though the *Hen House* and phased array radars also serve a vital dual role as part of the Soviet ABM forces.

The PKO consists of the Soviet anti-space defence service, and operates all anti-satellite and associated outer-space weapons systems. It does not appear that the Kola – for the moment – plays a major role for this service.

The PRO consists of the Soviet anti-rocket defences, or what we call Ballistic Missile Defence (BMD) forces. Considering the modernisation programme which this service has undergone since 1978 and the apparently considerable Soviet research and development effort in this field it would appear that it is an important part of the Vojska PVO.[11] The PRO comprises both the target acquisition radar systems and the actual interceptor missiles. In compliance with SALT the missiles are concentrated around Moscow and are not relevant to the Kola. On the other hand the target acquisition radars, without which the missiles are useless, are located to some extent in the Kola area. These include two older *Hen House* radars and the two new phased array radars in the Arkhangelsk Air Defence Sector.

Of these services important elements of the first, second, third and fifth services have been deployed to the Kola area. Here one should note that the Kola Peninsula is, for the Vojska PVO, part of the Arkhangelsk Air Defence Sector (AADS)[12], consisting of the same area as the NW TVD shown on Map 1.4. Since the Kola Vojska PVO forces are closely integrated in the overall Sector defence structure this section will deal with the sector as a whole and not with the Kola in isolation.

Table 2.5 shows the relative proportion of the total Vojska PVO services operating in the AADS. Here one should note again that exact numbers can vary, especially regarding the IA PVO and AEW forces, which can, within a relatively short time, be reinforced or concentrated in a given area. In this respect it is worth noting that the Kola airfield capacity far exceeds anything deployed to this area in peacetime. (See Part II.) However the statistics in the table do provide a rough indication of the relative importance of the AADS within the total Soviet strategic aerospace defence effort. It is clearly fairly high, with roughly one fifth of total Vojska PVO assets deployed here.

IA PVO	20% of IA PVO interceptors.
ZRV	6% of SAM systems.
RTV	46% of AEW aircraft.
	40% of phased array EW radars.
PRO	33% of Hen House target acquisition radars.

TABLE 2.5 The Relative Deployment to the
Arkhangelsk Air Defence Sector of Soviet Strategic
Air Defence Forces, 1985.

Vojska PVO Branch	Total USSR	Total AADS	Percentage AADS
Air Defence Districts/ Sectors	5	1	20%
Interceptors	1,200+	275	23%
SAM	1,200 (2)	70	6%
AEW	13	6	46%
EW radars (Phased Array)	5+	1	20%
(Hen House)	6 (3)	1	18%

Notes
(1) Arkhangelsk Air Defence Sector.
(2) This figure denotes SAM launch complexes, which each comprise several actual launchers.
(3) This figure denotes Hen House sites, each of which may house one or two radars.

Source: *The Military Balance 1985–1986*, p. 23.
Militaerbalansen 1985–1986, p. 132.

Summary, Strategic Forces

This section provides a general overview of Soviet primary strategic interests in the Kola area, as indicated by the deployment of Soviet strategic forces. The sources used indicate that roughly 20 per cent of Soviet offensive strategic nuclear forces are deployed to, or depend upon, Kola bases, and roughly 20 per cent of her defensive strategic forces are deployed to the Kola area. It is the deployment of these forces which provides the main source of Soviet military interest in the area, and the fact that roughly one fifth of her primary strategic assets depend upon the Kola indicate the level of this interest here.

SECONDARY THEATRE-LEVEL STRATEGIC SUPPORT FORCES AND THE KOLA.

In order to support the strategic interests in the Kola Peninsula the Soviet military has assigned a number of secondary forces to the area. Their main function is to protect the strategic forces' bases on the Kola, their operational concealment areas (for the SSBNs) and, to a lesser extent, their transit routes (for the DA). These secondary support forces consist of two main services.

The conventional forces of the Northern Fleet, with a primary responsibility for the security of the SSBN bases and operations areas, and defending Kola strategic bases from attack from the sea.
The IA PVO, ZRV and RTV of the Vojska PVO, however, in this role tasked with theatre air support of naval theatre operations, and possibly air support of amphibious and land frontal operations.

These forces, though strategically defensive when used for these tasks, have a pronounced regional role, and the prosecution of the strategic support missions cited above would involve considerable offensive operations on the theatre level in northern Fenno-scandia. This is because, from the Soviet perspective, the Kola assets would have to be defended in-depth in wartime, particularly insofar as naval operations are concerned. Such a strategic defence primarily involves two main theatre level operations. Defence against sea attack from the NATO naval theatre and tactical attack forces and defence against air attack from theatre and front level NATO aviation units. The first is mainly a naval task, while the second is mainly an air force task. (In addition both of these operations call for further air and ground operations along the Norwegian coastline and other littoral land areas and islands along the North Atlantic if they are to be successful. These are discussed on pages 36 to 38 as they are one step lower down on the list of strategic priorities, consisting of front and tactical level operations under the executive command of the Arctic Detached Front HQ.)

In the following two sections each of the two theatre support operations and forces will be outlined.

The Northern Fleet

The principal naval strategic support mission is the protection of the Kola bases and the operational concealment areas of the SSBNs from attack from the sea. This calls for extended defence-in-depth along the Atlantic, and involves three main operations off northern Fenno-scandia:

Deny the southern parts of the Norwegian Sea and northwards to NATO surface forces. The main forces are long range anti-shipping submarines and aircraft, and, under certain circumstances and when allocated by the General Staff, land and sea based theatre nuclear missiles.
Establish sufficient sea control of the central and northern parts of the Norwegian Sea to permit surface ASW task groups to operate there. The main forces are long/medium range anti-shipping aircraft, long/medium range air defence and anti-shipping surface vessels and – when so allocated by the General Staff – air defence aircraft from the IA PVO.
Carry out ASW defence-in-depth along the whole length of the Norwegian Sea to deny the Barents Sea and Greenland Basin to enemy submarines. The main forces for this task are long range ASW submarines (which would commence tracking and attack operations starting off the USN submarine bases on the United States East Coast and subsequently throughout the Atlantic), long and medium range ASW submarines operating in killing zones along the GIFUK gap and in the southern Norwegian Sea, long and medium range ASW surface task groups operating from the central Norwegian Sea northwards in conjunction with long range ASW aircraft, and, as of the northern Norwegian Sea, a very large force of medium to short range ASW surface vessels and aircraft operating from coastal bases.

These operations have as their primary objective the sealing off of the Kola from enemy naval attack forces and the sealing off of the Soviet 'SSBN Bastions' in Arctic waters, where the Soviet strategic nuclear

TABLE 2.6 The Relative Importance of the Kola
Peninsula as a Basing Area for the Various Elements
of the Conventional Portion of the Soviet Fleet,
1985. (1)

A.   Anti-submarine warfare forces. (2)

Type of Unit	Mission Range	Percentage Based on the Kola	
Submarines	Long range (SSN)	87%	(100%)
	Short range (SSK)	89%	(89%)
Surface vessels and aircraft	Long range (3)	60%	(83%)
	Medium range	34%	★
	Short range	17%	★

B.   Anti-surface shipping and air defence forces. (2)

Type of Unit	Mission Range	Percentage Based on the Kola	
Submarines	Long range (SSN/SSGN)	83%	(100%)
	Medium range (SSN)	66%	★
	Short range (SSG)	75%	★
	Short range (SS)	48%	(33%)
Surface vessels and aircraft	Long range (4)	76%	(100%)
	Medium range	34%	★
	Short range	32%	(0%)

C.   Amphibious assault vessels.

Type of Unit	Mission Range	Percentage Based on the Kola	
Surface vessels	Medium range	46%	★
	Short range	13%	★

Notes
The final percentage figure in brackets denotes the percentage of vessels of that particular type developed since 1980 which has been deployed to the Kola. This is important as it indicates the high qualitative priority of this area. In the event that an asterisk is shown (★) it means that no new ship types of this category have been developed since 1980.

(1) A detailed list of the exact ship categories and aircraft, along with their main armament, tonnage and range, is provided in the authors doctoral dissertation.

(2) This classification is based upon an analysis of the main type of armament with which the vessels are endowed as well as their designation in Soviet naval nomenclature. It is of course clear that no vessel is limited to one mission and, the larger the ship, the more flexible its assignment can be. However this table does serve to indicate the general priorities which Soviet naval planners have allocated to the Northern Fleet.

(3) A large portion of these vessels, by virtue of their size, also have a considerable secondary anti-surface shipping and/or air defence capability.

(4) This does not include those vessels already listed as having a primary ASW armament/classification orientation.

reserve, in the form of SSBNs, would be seeking to remain intact. However, though this is probably the main mission of the Soviet conventional fleet[13] this operations structure also permits the prosecution of a number of secondary missions, such as destroying enemy SSBNs and SSGNs operating north of the GIFUK gap, destroying NATO SLOC north of the GIFUK gap and providing cover for WAPA amphibious assault groups and resupply convoys.

Table 2.6 provides a rough overview of the percentage of Soviet long, medium and short range conventional naval forces deployed with the Northern Fleet. They are divided into two main types of forces, ASW and anti-surface shipping and air defence, according to their main weaponry and Soviet ship classification. However it is important to note that almost all larger Soviet surface vessels have an ASW capability, and that most of the larger vessels are flexible as to the types of mission they can carry out. Nonetheless the table does serve to indicate the considerable priority in terms of numbers, and especially in quality, of the conventional forces allocated to the Northern Fleet. As is mentioned in the table the forces listed include submarines, naval aviation aircraft (being ranked the second most important service in the Soviet conventional fleet) and surfaced vessels.

Finally however one should note that in addition to the present main task of defending the strategic assets on and around the Kola, the Northern Fleet would also have a second major theatre-level mission in wartime. This is the cutting of NATO trans-Atlantic SLOC in the central Atlantic. However the number of Northern Fleet forces which would be concentrated for this task is uncertain. Since NATO would be vitally dependent upon supplies and forces shipped across the Atlantic from the United States, the outcome of the Soviet Atlantic SLOC interdiction attempts could have a decisive effect on the battle for central Europe provided it remained non-nuclear. As such this mission is certainly important to the Soviet leadership. However, when seen from the broader strategic perspective the cutting of NATO Atlantic SLOC is not as important as the preservation of the strategic SSBN nuclear reserve. Thus it would appear quite certain that the protection of SSBN missions has priority, and that the bulk of the Northern Fleet assets would be directed towards this end. The number of assets assigned to central Atlantic anti-SLOC operations would therefore depend upon how many could be spared from the SSBN defence operations. It is incidentally very much along these lines of reasoning that the USN 'Maritime Strategy', with forward defence operations involving tracking and attacking Soviet SSBNs in wartime, is based, the ostensible purpose of the USN anti-SSBN orientation being to force the Soviet Navy to draw back its forces for their defence, thereby reducing the number of forces it can free for the central Atlantic anti-SLOC operations.

In any event, however, it is clear that the Northern Fleet conventional forces have been receiving the majority of vessels in most of their mission types, and also the highest proportion of modern vessels. In all likelihood this pattern will remain constant in the coming years. It could also increase, as the United

States Navy emphasis upon maritime 'forward defence' could enable those factions within the Soviet military who support a larger conventional fleet to argue convincingly that, because the threat to the SSBNs is increasing the fleet requires more ships to protect them. This could lead to greater allocations of resources to naval construction than would otherwise have been the case.

Vojska PVO forces in the strategic support role.

Since the general force breakdown of the Vojska PVO on the Kola already has been provided, this section will be limited to an outline of the secondary strategic support missions of this service in the north-west. These consist primarily of providing air cover for the Northern Fleet conventional forces in their battle for the North Atlantic. Secondly, and on a lower level of priority, they consist of providing air cover for the tactical support forces of the Independent Far Northern Front in their attempts to neutralise or occupy areas of Northern Norway and possibly northern Sweden and Finland in time of war. However it is important at this stage to emphasise that these missions, through performed by the same service, are strictly subordinate to the primary strategic aerospace role. It is the duty of the Stavka VGK to determine, in consultation with the GK VPVO and on the basis of its direct operational command of the Arctic Detached Front and the Northern Fleet, when and to what extent the Vojska PVO theatre capable forces are to be allocated to these subordinate roles. This is one of the reasons why as a high a level of centralised command from the Stavka VGK is retained for the northwestern forces. Because this is the optimal and most rapid way that decisions can be made allocating air support from the Vojska PVO to assist the theatre and frontal forces in the northwest, while minimising the danger to strategic readiness. By retaining direct operational command of the Arctic Detached Front and the Northern Fleet, and indirect operational command of the IA PVO through the GK VPVO, the Stavka VGK is able immediately to assess the requirements of the situation and, through its Vojska PVO channels, call for air control support if the strategic situation, which it again is in direct contact with, permits.

On this level the main Vojska PVO missions would be to provide air cover during critical phases of the battle for northern Norway and the Norwegian Sea, and for high-value friendly combatants. These air support operations of the Vojska PVO are vital if the strategic bases and resources on the Kola are to be protected. This is mainly due to the lack of sufficient independent air defence aircraft in the Northern Fleet conventional force combined with the considerable capabilities – both offensive and defensive – of the United States carrier-borne aircraft. The only aircraft presently under the Soviet naval command for this purpose, the Yak-36 *Forger*, are neither present in sufficient numbers nor possess the capabilities required for more than pinpoint and very temporary air defence operations in the Atlantic OTVD. Nor will the deployment of the first Soviet through-deck carrier later in this decade significantly alter this picture. Firstly because it will take a number of years before the operational experience can be acquired for carrier air operations to be effective, and secondly because there will still remain an overwhelming NATO naval air superiority in the air control field in the northern Atlantic.

Thus for the present and foreseeable future the Atlantic OTVD will be dependent upon receiving land based air defence support from the IA PVO at the very least during key battles and stages of the theatre operations. To a lesser extent the same applies to the front level forces of the Arctic Detached Front. While these have some integral ground-based air defence capability, their main Army air defence units are integrated in the Vojska PVO ZRV. For key operations, such as theatre attack on Norwegian airfields and key defence targets by elements of the 24 Air Army, or, on a lower level, amphibious assault operations, portions of the IA PVO and ZRV would probably be required for support. The priority of these latter operations, however, being on the frontal level, would be lower than the theatre naval air support and air strike operations.

TERTIARY FRONT-LEVEL THEATRE SUPPORT FORCES AND THE KOLA.

On the lowest level the Soviet Union has deployed front level tactical support forces to the Kola, with the main purpose of providing support for the naval and Vojska PVO forces in their secondary theatre operations in the far north.

These Front level forces consist of an operational Frontal HQ probably under the direct command of the Stavka VGK via the General Staff.[14] The Front HQ is in combined command of forces from two of the main peacetime administrative military services (the Ground Forces and Air Forces) in the Leningrad Military District. The combined Frontal command includes:

1.   From the Ground Forces.
     SV (*Sukhoputnyye Vojska*)

       Motorised Rifle Troops.
       MV (*Motostrelkovyye Vojska*)

       Rocket Troops and Artillery.
       RViA (*Raketnyye Vojska i Artillerija*)

       Tactical Air Assault Forces.

       Special Forces.
       Reydoviki, Vysotniki, Front-level *Spetsnaz*, etc.

2   From the Air Forces.
     VVS (*Voyenno-Vozdushnyye Sily*)

       Frontal Aviation Forces (from the VVS)
       FA (*Frontaja Aviatsija*)

Army Aviation (from the VVS).
AA (*Armejskaja Aviatsija*)

3   From the Navy.
VMF (*Voyenno Morskaja Flota*)

Amphibious Assault Forces.
MP (*Morskaja Pekhota*)

It is worth noting that the administrative unit 'Tank Troops' (Tankovyye Vojska) is not included here as there are no larger tank formations in the Leningrad Military District.

These are under the direct command of the Arctic Detached Front HQ and probably in wartime would be organised into one Front, consisting of the Leningrad MD Frontal Aviation Forces, the 6 Army Group (facing Norwegian and Finnish Lappland), the 30 Army Corps (Viborg) and the 27 Army Corps (Arkhangelsk).

In addition a number of further forces can be assigned to support the Far Northern Independent Front commander by the General Staff. These include some of those forces which are under the direct operational command of the Stavka VGK:

Theatre bomber force.
DA (Dal'nyaja Aviatsija)

Theatre airborne forces.
Parachute Divisions, VDV (Vozdushno-Desantnyye Vojska)

Strategic Transport Aviation.
VTA (Voyenno-Transportnaja Aviatsija).

Centrally controlled GRU Spetsnaz formations.

Depending upon the need in the north in relation to other operational areas, as well as the overall war plan, the Stavka VGK would decide which and how many units from each of the above might assist the Arctic Detached Front Commander.

The main purpose of the Arctic Detached Front is threefold, and includes:

Direct defence of the Kola bases from land and amphibious attack.

Support for the Vojska PVO in its strategic air defence task, by neutralising or occupying NATO forward land-based surveillance installations and airfields in northern Norway.

Support for the Northern Fleet conventional forces battle for the north Atlantic, by neutralising or occupying NATO forward land based surveillance installations, airfields, harbours and coastal areas in northern Norway.

The main level of ambition of the Arctic Detached Front operations in wartime would in all likelihood lie at some point on a scale between the minimum requirement to deny use of northern Norway to NATO, and the maximum objective of acquiring it for Soviet use. In both cases a mix of ground and air operations would be involved. In addition attempts would be made to neutralise NATO bases in central and south Norway. This would probably primarily take place through Spetsnaz and air attack operations as, at least in the early phases of a war (the first few weeks), a land invasion of these areas from the north is almost Utopian. This is not to say, however, that an attempt could not be made, using the Baltic Detached Front to force its way through southern Sweden, or a combined Baltic Detached Front and Northern Front

thrust through Denmark. Again however this notion seems unlikely at least in the early stages of a war. However, much depends upon the extent to which Sweden, Norway and Denmark are paralysed by Spetsnaz operations at the outset of a conflict.

The minimum objective of the Far Northern Independent Front calls for preventing NATO forces from being able to use northern Norway as a springboard for air, sea or even (at a later stage in a war) land/amphibious attacks against the Kola. This minimum scenario would involve two main combined operations:

Basically defensive ground operations, with a limited advance into the relatively undefended Norwegian Finnmark, stopping short of the Norwegian Troms defence concentrations, and no ground moves through Finland or Sweden. The main objective would be to acquire depth for the defences and to draw as few frontal forces as possible from the Western TVD. Thus only forces from the Leningrad MD would be used, and Stavka VGK strategic and theatre support forces – such as the Parachute Divisions or the Strategic Transport Aviation – would not be allocated.

A very offensive and of necessity sustained level of air operations over Norway. This would involve heavy overflights of Swedish and Finnish airspace, and constant bombing of Norwegian airfields and other key military installations in northern and, on a lower rate of intensity, southern, Norway. The purpose would be to keep NATO installations out of operation so that NATO could not attack the Kola from this area, nor support the battle for the North Atlantic. These offensive theatre air operations would involve the whole of the Far Northern Front tactical aviation, and would also require a considerable input from the theatre bomber forces of the Stavka VGK, reducing their availability for the Western TVD.

In the maximalist scenario the responsibility for achieving the theatre objective would lie with the frontal forces, with the theatre air units playing a relatively more subdued role. This would involve:

Offensive front-level land, sea and tactical air operations with the objective of actually occupying key military areas in northern Norway. This would have the dual effect of denying them to NATO and, perhaps, of permitting their use by Soviet forces. This includes both the occupation of forward airfields to support the air strike and air defence requirements of the Atlantic OTVD, and the need to provide dispersed and forward basing for naval forces in the Norwegian fjords. These operations would probably require support from the Baltic Military District, as well as allocations of theatre airborne and amphibious forces by the Stavka VGK. It could draw quite heavily from the resources required for the Western TVD. Such operations would also probably involve attempts to cross northern Finland and Sweden overland, and maintain logistic lines of communications through these areas.

Relatively limited offensive theatre air operations, probably restricted to an initial very heavy air strike to assist the offensive of the ground forces. Subsequently the responsibility for keeping the NATO bases harmless would lie with the frontal forces and their attempts to occupy them physically. This would have the advantage of permitting more intensive theatre air operations in the Western TVD.

These two possibilities represent two extreme options, and actual events could lie at some point between them or combine the most passive or most active ingredients from both. It is worth noting that it is generally not considered possible to prevent air operations from NATO airfields for more than a limited space of time if only air strikes are used. Thus, from this point of view, the actual occupation of northern Norway seems necessary. However this must be balanced against the difficulties such an operation entails, and the costs, in terms of diversion northwards of scale resources. Something which is not generally recognised in the west is the enormous difficulty which any army would have of actually crossing the 400 kilometres (as the crow flies between Skibotn and the Alakurtti border) of Finnish Lappland. Perhaps the fighting spearhead could force its way through, but its logistic tail could almost certainly not survive. And after some time the fighting spearhead would run out of supplies, after which it would rapidly lose its fighting strength. Thus a large scale land invasion of northern Norway through the neutrals is a very doubtful proposition at best.

The important point however is to note the rationale behind these scenarios. This basically rests on the need for frontal operations in northern Fenno–scandia to support the Vojska PVO and/or Atlantic OTVD. There is no actual advantage *per se* of occupying northern Norway or even all of northern Fenno–scandia, and the justification for diverting scarce land and air resources for operations here is entirely a function of their contribution to the aerospace and naval strategic and theatre operations. This is an additional reason why there is no such thing as a 'Northern TVD'. The area quite simply is not important enough on its own terms. Thus, were a TVD to be established it would have to come under a naval or Vojska PVO command, since it is these theatres which the land operations in the far north are designed to support, and not the other way around. This is also something which it is highly doubtful that the influential Ground Forces contingent in the General Staff would permit.

REFERENCES

1. HINES, John G. and Phillip A. PETERSEN: 'Changing the Soviet System of Control: Focus on theatre warfare.' *International Defense Review*, Vol. 19, No. 3, March 1986: p. 287.

    POLMAR, Norman: *Guide to the Soviet Navy*. Annapolis, Naval Institute Press, 3rd. rev. ed., 1983: p. 10.

    SCOTT, Harriet Fast and William F.: 'Command Structure.' *United States Naval Institute Proceedings*, Vol. 111/12/994, December 1985: p. 42.

    SCOTT, William F.: 'Organisation of the Soviet Armed Forces.' *Air Force Magazine*, Vol. 69, No. 3, March 1986: p. 74.

    'Soviet Intelligence: Chernavin. The New C in C of the Soviet Navy.' *Jane's Defence Weekly*, January 18, 1986: pp. 61-2.

2. HEMSLEY, John G.: *Soviet Troop Control*, London, Brassey's Defence Publishers Ltd., 1st. ed., 1982: p. 44.

    HINES and PETERSEN: 'Changing the Soviet . . .', op. cit., p. 287.

    The Military Balance 1985–1986. London, The International Institute for Strategic Studies, 1985: p.21.

SCOTT and SCOTT: 'Command Structure.', op. cit., p. 42.

SCOTT, William F.: 'Organisation of the . . .', op. cit., p. 74.

Soviet Military Power 1986. Washington D.C., Department of Defense, 5th. ed., March 1986: p. 31.

3. MccGWIRE, Michael: 'The Rationale for the Development of Soviet Seapower.' *United States Naval Institute Proceedings*, Vol. 106, No. 5, May 1980: pp. 155–183.

4. See for instance.

    BALL, Desmond: 'Nuclear War at Sea.' *International Security*, Vol. 10, No. 3, Winter 1985–1986: pp. 3–31.

    BESNAULT, Réne: 'Un nouveau théatre d'opérations sous marines: Pénétration de l'Arctique.' *Stratégique*, 2ième trimestre 1981: pp. 51–86.

    BUOB, Jacques: 'Sous-marins: la guerre du silence.' *L'Express*, 22/7-83: 30.

    The Guardian, 17/7-83.

    Los Angeles Times, 12/9-80, p. 1.

    MEACHAM, James: 'Down Under.' *The Economist*, April 19, 1986: pp. 58–59.

    POSEN, Barry R.: 'Inadvertent Nuclear War? Escalation and NATO's Northern Flank.' *International Security*, Vol. 7, No. 2, Fall 1982: pp. 28–54.

    RIES, Tomas: *The Evolution of the Nordic Military-Strategic Environment 1955–1985 and the Consequences for Regional Stability*. Geneva, Unpublished draft of doctoral dissertation, 20/12-85: pp. 310–317.

    SPAVEN, Malcolm: 'ELF: Surviving the Traumas. Part II.' *Jane's Defence Weekly*, Vol. 4, No. 22, 30/11-85: pp. 1194–1197.

    ULSAMER, Edgar: 'Bobbing, Weaving and Fighting Smart. The US Navy looks to new systems and to new concepts to maintain its maritime edge.' *Air Force Magazine*, August 1983: pp. 88–93.

5. See references above, notably:

    RIES, T.: *The Evolution . . .*, pp. 310 –317.

6. 'Soviet Air Force Re-equipment.' *Jane's Defence Review*, Vol. 4, No. 3, 1984: pp. 249–251.

7. One should note that the Tu-26 *Backfire* B – when taking into account its aerial refuelling potential – is considered by the Pentagon as an intercontinental range strategic nuclear bomber.

8. ARKIN William M. and Richard W. FIELDHOUSE: *Nuclear Battlefields. Global Links in the Arms Race*. Cambridge, Ma., Ballinger Publishing Co., 1st. ed., 1985: p. 43.

    Militaerbalansen 1984 –1985. Ed. by Ellman ELLINGSEN, Oslo, The Norwegian Atlantic Committee, 1985: p. 98.

9. The acronym SIOP stands for 'Single Integrated Operational Plan', grouping together the triad of United States strategic nuclear forces (ICBMs, long range strategic bombers and SSBNs) and assigning them their various missions as part of a strategic nuclear attack on the Soviet Union. Some books dealing with this topic are:

    BRACKEN, Paul: *The Command and Control of Nuclear Forces*. New Haven, Conn., Yale University Press, 1st. ed., 1983.

PRINGLE, Peter and William ARKIN: *SIOP: The Secret US Plan for Nuclear War*. New York, NY, W. W. Norton, 1st. ed., 1983.

10. SCOTT, Harriet Fast and William F.: *The Armed Forces of the USSR*. Boulder, Co., Westview Press, 1st. ed., 1979: p. 147. ('Troops of the National Air Defense. Vojska Protivovozdushnoy Oborony Strany – PVO Strany.')

     'Air Defense.' *Soviet Military Power 1986*. Washington, D.C., Department of Defense, 5th ed., March 1986: pp. 53–57.

11. 'Ballistic Missile Defence.' *Soviet Military Power 1986*. Washington, D.C., Department of Defense, 5th. ed., March 1986: pp. 42–48.

12. KORKISCH, Friedrich: 'Die heimatluftverteidigung der Sowjetunion,' *Osterreichische Militärische Zeitschrift*, XXII Jahrgang, Heft 3, 1984: pp. 223–228.

13. For a very thorough examination of this issue see:

     RIES, Tomas: 'The Evolution of Soviet Naval Interests, Forces and Operations in the Nordic Region 1948–1985.' *The Evolution of the Nordic Military-Strategic Environment 1955–1985 and the Consequences for Regional Stability*. Geneva, Draft of the doctoral dissertation, 20/12-85: pp. 217–345.

14. SUVOROV, V.: 'Strategic Command and Control: The Soviet Approach.' *International Defense Review*, Vol. 17, No. 12, December 1984: pp. 1816–1817.

CHAPTER 3

Conclusion

For the last two decades there has been a growing general awareness of the strategic importance of the Kola Peninsula, and a vague recognition that it plays a major role in the security of the Nordic states. Unfortunately a systematic and thorough understanding of why this should be so has hitherto been absent. With the above presentation hopefully this gap has been bridged and the reader may perhaps have gained a better understanding of what the Soviet military has placed on the Kola, why they have placed it there, and what the implications are in terms of wartime scenarios and Soviet perceptions.

Such an understanding is actually vitally important for all the inhabitants of the five Nordic countries, as the Soviet strategic interests represented on the Kola are one of the main determinants of the security and stability of the Nordic region. While it is all very well to note that the general level of Soviet forces in the North Atlantic and adjacent areas may be growing, this does not help us very much when trying to understand why this should be so. And without such an understanding it is very difficult to judge what future developments may take place and, especially, what the consequences of our actions and reactions will be in terms of Soviet policy in the area.

The preceding analysis has attempted to provide the factual basis permitting such an analysis. The report is not intended to draw any explicit conclusions, but rather to provide a basis for understanding the Soviet military interest in her north-western area. From this the following main points should be clear about the military/strategic situation of the Nordic states from the Soviet-military perspective:

The Nordic states are *not* a strategically vital Soviet military target. The real northern focus of Soviet strategic interest lies in the Arctic, both as an SSBN sanctuary and as a forward strategic air defence zone.

Portions of the nordic states *do* constitute important Soviet military targets in time of wartime. To support the Arctic strategic interests, and particularly to protect the SSBN assets, the Soviet Union would have to engage in secondary operational missions in the north Atlantic and adjacent areas. To support these operations the Soviet armed forces would have to operate on the frontal level against key areas in Norway, probably through Sweden and Finland. Such operations could either be denial-oriented, involving sustained bombing and other destruction operations, or use-

oriented, involving the actual occupation of key areas.

This means that under all circumstances parts of the Nordic area are of conventional military interest to the Soviet Union. This has led to the deployment of Soviet military forces in the region which have a decidedly local orientation and affect the regional military situation. So far the Nordic military efforts have roughly balanced the Soviet forces and one might speak of a rough military equilibrium in the area on the tactical level.

However, Soviet front-level military assets in the north are constantly improving, especially in terms of the quality of air and ground forces equipment and with the introduction of helicopter and special forces to the area. Under these circumstances, if the Nordic states are to retain a credible defence, it is vital that their military forces keep pace. In practical terms this means that defence capability will have to be kept up by consistent increases in the defence budget.

An additional factor is that, should the pressure on Soviet strategic interests in the Arctic increase, it is conceivable that Soviet regional military conventional forces will increase over and above their normal rate of modernisation and present rough numerical stability. This could present a problem for the regional military equilibrium. If the Soviet Union perceives that her SSBN forces are a vital national security asset, and if she perceives they are seriously threatened, funds and resources might be channelled towards a major build-up of the Northern Fleet and possibly towards further air and ground forces for the Kola. The United States Maritime Strategy, as presented officially in January 1986, is in fact explicitly placing Soviet SSBNs at risk.

This is not necessarily meant as a critique of the Maritime Strategy which has to be seen in a far greater context. However it does mean that we in the north must be aware of the possible consequences. Firstly, if this leads to major increases in Soviet force levels in the northwest, it could place considerable pressure on the Nordic states. Unless such a development were matched by increased defence efforts in the Nordic countries it could lead to a military imbalance *vis-a-vis* the Soviet Union, which, while it would probably not lead to an isolated Soviet attack on any of the Nordic states, could well have considerable political repercussions. Particularly the maritime situation in the Norwegian Sea in peacetime is important. Should the Northern Fleet establish a predominant and permanent presence here it could contribute towards isolating the Nordic area, and would call for an increased and visible Western naval presence. If Soviet theatre and front level air and ground forces in the Leningrad Military District are significantly raised it would threaten the defence credibility of present Norwegian, Swedish and Finnish forces.

Secondly, and this seems less speculative, the situation will lead to a more tense strategic environment next to Fenno–scandia. United States naval pressure on Soviet SSBNs, coupled with both sides growing focus upon strategic long range bombers and their Arctic air routes, increase the sources for local tension. With an increasing superpower focus upon this area the Nordic states and their populations will have to learn to live with and manage a peacetime situation which is far more unstable and tense than what they have become accustomed to in earlier postwar decades. In this sense an increased preparedness for crisis management in the Nordic region will probably have to be made.

Finally, it is important to note that the present study has been limited to assessing the Soviet military wartime interests in Fenno–scandia and adjacent areas. It thereby does not cover Soviet peacetime interests in the area, nor – and this is perhaps one of the most important areas – the potential peacetime implications for nordic stability of the evolving military environment. This is a subject of its own and for the time being it is probably enough to note merely that the time of low regional tension is over and we must be prepared to make the mental and psychological adjustments required for the difficult times ahead.

Part 2

The Soviet Military Basing Infrastructure on the Kola Peninsula

TOMAS RIES and JOHNNY SKORVE

THE SATELLITE STUDY OF THE KOLA PENINSULA

This section is based upon an analysis of available open information which we have compared with the satellite pictures of the Kola area. This has permitted us with a fair degree of accuracy to verify the claims of the various published reports on military installations on the Kola. In addition it has allowed us to identify entirely new facilities on the Kola, as well as locate certain installations whose position was previously not publicly known. Finally, through a close examination of the photographs, we have been able to acquire detailed data about certain installations, naval underground facilities, SAM missile sites, and so forth.

Two new military developments of major interest are identified in this report. The first is the present construction of a new very large airfield by the river Schagui, and the second is the recent completion of a very large and mainly underground naval base next to Gremikha. It must be stressed, however, that they do not in any way indicate a radical increase in the threat to, for instance, Norway, or increased aggressive intentions by the Soviet Union. They should rather be seen as part of the steady development and modernisation of the Soviet military forces, just as in the West. However, this said, one should note that this long term development, and especially any increase of the strategic basing on the Kola, does make the strategic situation for the Nordic states more difficult. In this broader context these new Soviet bases are significant.

The Schagui Airfield

The most visible new significant development on the Kola is the construction of a new, very large airfield by the river Schagui, next to the Bay of Kandalaksha. The construction work is quite clearly visible (see Map 5.1 and especially Plate 7.3 and the accompanying text) from the satellites. This airfield is significant in that it appears to be very large. The runway is estimated as 4,600 metres, which will make it equivalent to the longest runway presently operational on the Kola, the strategic bomber Forward Operating Location (FOL) at Olenegorsk, also with 4,600 metres. The length of the runway, as well as its location, indicates that it may be intended as a strategic intercontinental bomber airbase or FOL, which also fits in well with the forthcoming operational deployment of the *Blackjack* strategic bomber. The Schagui development is examined closer in Section 4.

The Gremikha Naval Base

The second interesting new development is the major harbour complex in the vicinity of Gremikha. This is located on the northern coastline of the Kola, but as far east as is possible considering ice conditions. The satellite pictures show that a very large harbour has been constructed here. This appears to include several very long quays and elaborate harbour facilities, as well as fixed SAM sites overlooking the base. This, as well as certain open sources, indicates that the Gremikha complex is probably constructed specifically for the new large Soviet submarines, such as the *Oscar* class. However it does not seem as if the Gremikha facilities have supported the *Typhoon* SSBN class. This development is examined closer in pages 55 to 63.

In addition to these major visible developments a number of other installations have been identified, whose locations, and in some cases existence, were not previously known. These include the extension of the already relatively large road network in the major basing area for ground forces between Murmansk and the Norwegian border, the nuclear weapons arsenal by Severomorsk, the aged nuclear missile silo complex by Revda, possibly the Murmansk nuclear power plant (located virtually in the centre of Murmansk), an entirely new hydro-electric power station by Teriberka some seventy kilometres east of Murmansk, the Murmansk dry dock purchased from Sweden, and so forth.

However the most interesting part of the study has been the ability to confirm the relatively uncertain open reports on the Kola military basing infrastructure, combined with the possibility to examine these bases in detail. In the following pages the general results of this study are presented, together with an analysis of selected specific bases.

MILITARY AND CIVIL SATELLITE REMOTE SENSING

In the late 1950s[1] satellite observation of the earth became increasingly important, with meteorological satellites providing the first systematic global observations. However at that time the need for reliable information on Soviet ICBM deployments strongly accelerated the development of United States military satellite reconnaissance. In February 1958 President Eisenhower authorised the start of a reconnaissance satellite program, and only a year later the first *Discoverer* satellite was launched. These photosatellites had cameras on board photographing selected areas within the Soviet Union.

The exposed films are transferred to protective capsules that are later ejected from the satellite. After penetrating the earth's atmosphere, the film capsules are caught in mid air by specially equipped aircraft, as they float by parachute through the lower part of the atmosphere; or they are sometimes picked up by frogmen from the ocean surface.

During 1961 *Discoverer* satellites provided American military intelligence with the first detailed coverage of a Soviet ICBM site. The quality of United States military photo-reconnaisssance during the first decade of operation has never been revealed, but a similar camera system from Itec Corporation was used on Apollo missions to the moon. From an altitude of 100 kilometres photographs of the lunar surface show details as small as one metre across.

The military requirement for satellite photo-reconnaissance in the United States is so varied that different types of satellite are used. One type is designed to observe large areas of land and ocean to search for and find activities of military significance. This was the main objective for the early *Discoverer* satellites.

Today the United States operates the following military earth-observing satellites:

KH-8: 3rd generation 'close-look' satellites.
KH-9: 4th generation area surveillance imaging satellites. ('Big Bird')
KH-11: 1st generation real-time digital imaging satellites.

These all move in polar orbits, enabling them to observe practically the whole of the earth's surface.

The *KH-8*s move in sun-synchronous orbits and thus observe the different regions of the world at the same local time in the same way as the civil satellites like *Landsat* and *Spot* do. The 'close-look' satellites are flying eighty day missions with apogee/perigee maximum and minimum distance from the earth's surface of 350/120 kilometres. The spacecraft is cylindric, 17.7 metres long and 1.5 metres in diametre, weighing 3500 kilogrammes.

It is not possible for a reasonable period of time to obtain a stable satellite orbit any lower than 120 kilometres because the atmospheric drag will force them down rapidly, thereby burning them up in the atmosphere. The best pictures from these satellites have a ground resolution of approximately 10 centimetres.

The *KH-9* photographs land and ocean regions of military interest. The film is processed on board and the developed pictures are scanned systematically and transmitted to earth. 'Big Bird' satellites also release capsules containing exposed film that are returned to earth for direct processing in the same way as described for the *Discoverer* satellite. *KH-9* is 15.25 metres long and 3.1 metres wide with a weight of 13,600 kilogrammes. Like the *KH-8*, this type also moves in a sun-synchronous orbit with apogee/perigee of 250/160 kilometres. 'Big Bird' satellites carry four returnable film capsules, as opposed to the two capsules carried on the *KH-8*.

The *KH-11* satellites use a similar method of image transmission as the *Landsat* and *Spot* satellites. The images are converted by the sensors into sets of digital values which represent the levels of illumination of the individual picture elements (pixels). These values are transmitted to ground stations as real time information shortly after passing over areas of interest. The *KH-11* do not quite provide the same very high resolution images as the 'close-look' satellites. However *KH-8* has limited amounts of film and ejectable capsules for returning exposed film to the earth. The

strength of *KH-11*s is their long operational lifetime and multispectral imaging. The record-breaking *KH-11* satellite had a lifetime of 770 days and thus generated a number of images several magnitudes greater than the capacity of a *KH-8*. With *KH-11* full advantage is also taken of computerised digital interpretation possible.

Systematic non-military satellite imaging of the earth surface started in 1972 with the *Landsat* earth resources technology satellite system. The initial *Landsat* series *1* to *3*, operating during the period 1972-82, used the MSS-scanner and the RBV-television systems. One such *Landsat* scene covers 185 × 185 kilometres of the earth's surface and the satellite takes four simultaneous multispectral pictures of the same area, two in the visible and two in the near infrared part of spectrum.

The smallest area on the ground visible on these *Landsat* pictures is 57 × 79 metres. In 1982 NASA launced an improved version, *Landsat 4*, that in addition to the MMS-scanner, has one new imaging instrument, the Thematic Mapper (TM). It has a ground resolution of 30 metres and simultaneous registration in seven spectral bands. Presently only *Landsat 5* is transmitting TM-data.

In February 1986 France launched their first earth observing satellite, *Spot*. It operates in two different modes: carrying out multispectral registration in three bands with 20 metre resolution, or taking panchromatic (black and white) pictures with 10 metre resolution. This means that with the *Spot* images one is able to obtain the most detailed panchromatic images of ground objects so far available with civil resources.

In remote sensing, the smallest area on ground that can be registered with a camera or scanner instrument on board a satellite is known as a 'picture element', or 'pixel' for short. The smaller the pixel can be made, the more detailed an image one can get. One single *Landsat* MSS image is made up of about seven and a half million pixels where each of these is given a greytone-value between 0 and 255, with 0 for white and black for 255.

Only objects larger than the pixel size will be detected however, as each pixel essentially only consists of a square block with a single panchromatic tone somewhere on the scale between 0 and 255. For identification the object must therefore be six to nine times larger than the pixel size, and to be able to make a description of an object it must be even larger than for mere identification. This can explain why military close-look satellites must provide pixel sizes down to the ten centimetre range.

Each digital satellite image, military or civil, consists of millions of pixels. The number of pixels in an image can vary somewhat. However if we simplify the situation by assuming that all digital images have the same information content, then the aerial coverage of the earth's surface becomes a function of the resolution: i.e. of the pixel size. The relatively low resolution of the *Landsat* MSS-scanner has picture-scenes each covering 185 × 185 kilometres = 34,000 square kilometres. Theoretically if we could improve the *Landsat* MSS images to have a ground resolution of 10 metres, and simultaneously keep the information content unchanged, the scene would be reduced to 23 × 23 kilometres = 529 square kilometres.

Generally speaking, the rule is that the finer the pixels are, the smaller the area that can be covered. Military 'close-look' satellites, like *KH-8*, cover only small areas. If, for example, a pixel size of 30 × 30 centimetres is applied one such satellite scene covers approximately 2,270 × 2,270 metres of the earth's surface. Thus 7,500 × 7,500, or 56 million pixels, are needed for imaging just this small area measuring 5.2 square kilometres. To cover larger areas with such very high resolution presents several problems due to the enormous processing load the satellite sensors would generate.

Normally satellite imaging takes place as cameras or other sensors scan those areas directly below the satellite (nadir). As the satellite moves, a strip of earth located vertically below the orbit is imaged. Thus in the course of one observation cycle, the whole of the earth's surface has been imaged. During each pass of *Landsat* 4 and 5, their sensors cover a 185 kilometre broad swath with an observation cycle of sixteen days. The *Spot* satellite has two HRV instruments, each covering 60 × 60 kilometres. Oriented perpendicularly to the orbit, they provide a combined swath of 117 kilometres as the two fields overlap by three kilometres. The *Spot* observation cycle is twenty-six days.

It would be impossible for military 'close-look' satellites to acquire coverage of critical areas quickly if imaging was restricted to nadir-pointing sensors, even with quite frequent repositioning of the orbit. This is solved by oblique viewing, carried out by making the cameras or imaging sensors able to look to either side of the orbit. This can be done by changing the orientation of a pointing mirror which is controlled from the ground. Therefore the observed sites or regions need not be centred on the ground track of the satellite's orbit. This 'side-looking' capability, combined with high precision pointing control, enables satellites of this type to image high priority and critical areas quickly. It also has the advantage of making it much more difficult for a foe to predict which areas are under satellite observation at a given time. This makes concealment efforts, based on avoiding exposure of sensitive assets at given times, virtually impossible. Off-nadir imaging also makes it possible to obtain stereoscopic pictures of interesting regions. By taking two or more pictures from different angles, stereo pairs are produced and the interpreters are thereby provided with a three-dimensional viewing of

an area, permitting stereoscopic analysis and detailed studies.

Prior to the spate of accidents of the Space Shuttle, *Titan* 34D and *Delta* rockets during the winter of 1986, it was expected that the first of a new generation of photo reconnaissance satellites, the *KH-12*, was to have been launched later this year. The difference between this new system and the *KH-11* is improved resolution. *KH-12* is expected to provide as detailed images as those of the 'close-look' *KH-8* satellites. It is expected that Space Shuttle will launch the 14,500 kilo *KH-12*, and also retrieve its predecessor for refurbishment on the ground.

THE USE OF SATELLITE TECHNOLOGY IN THE PRESENT STUDY

Satellite remote sensing technology is a valuable tool for acquiring information on foreign areas when on-site inspection is not possible. In this study satellite remote sensing has been used for this purpose. The existence of the Kola military installations, and their development over time, is of vital strategic concern for the future security of Norway and indeed of all adjacent states in northern Europe, such as Iceland, Finland and Sweden. At the same time, however, information on the Kola developments has been very limited, and when available in open sources, of uncertain value. By employing satellite technology we have been able to verify existing open information on the military installations and activities on the Kola, and make our own independent examination of areas and bases so far overlooked. This has permitted us, to a limited extent, both to weed out false existing information and to supply new information, in certain cases, such as the Schagui airfield and Gremikha naval base.

In this study, satellite images spread over an interval of almost thirteen years – from July 1973 to August 1985 – have been used. This has also permitted us to make studies over a period of the temporal development of the Kola military infrastructure.

One should note that *Landsat* thematic mapper pictures of the Kola first became available in 1985. Therefore it has not been possible to observe any detailed change over time using civil satellites prior to the launching of *Landsat* 5 in 1985. However larger scale changes, such as the construction of roads, and the like, have been observed with *Landsat* satellites since 1973.

On the technical level, two types of satellite images have been used: *Landsat* MSS and *Landsat* TM. With the considerable range in pixel sizes, they differ much with respect to the information content. Finally one should note that due to the cost the third available civil satellite resource, *Spot*, was not used, though its panchromatic images are about fifty times more detailed than the *Landsat* MSS pictures.

What can be seen on these three types of satellite

imagery, can in a general way be described by some typical features found on the Kola Peninsula.

Landsat MSS: (Fifty-seven by seventy-nine metres resolution)
Roads, towns, medium-sized populated areas, harbours and air-fields. Also seen are major changes that have taken place over time like the expansion of urban areas and the building of new roads and airfields.

Landsat TM: (Thematic Mapper – thirty metres resolution)
Jetties in harbours, small roads, railroad tracks and the runway pattern on airfields.

Spot: (Ten metres resolution)
These pictures show great similarities with high altitude aerial photographs. In towns the street pattern and separate buildings are obvious. Finer details can be seen in harbours and protective shelters for military airplanes.

To assist in the interpretation and analysis of the satellite imagery special photo-optical methods and image processing techniques were used. The measurements were made with the use of a computer-assisted Hewlett-Packard digitizer.

The availability of new, high resolution images from TM and *Spot* have also had the favourable feedback effect of making it possible to perform a more detailed interpretation of the older MSS pictures. This has been possible by exploiting the new knowledge and deeper understanding of the area obtained by the new satellite information. The use of

TM data also proved to be valuable in gaining new and additional insight into the area by considering the effects of temporal changes in the images. With respect to the Kola pictures the changes include differences in vegetation intensity, variation in shadowing due to sun elevation and changes in appearance of the landscape when it is snow-covered.

The use of temporal registration has also provided an insight into the tempo and timing of the sometimes considerable activities on the Kola. One good example is the important roadwork west of Murmansk. During the summer of 1985 favourable weather resulted in cloud-free TM images taken only sixteen days apart. When these two scenes were analysed and compared it was possible to discern the increased intensity of roadwork during this period. Measurements indicated that during these sixteen days top soil along a stretch one thousand metres long had been removed by road-equipment along the planned extension of the new road. The same two TM-scenes also clearly reveal changes in the number and position of the many ships in the Murmansk fjord. It is also possible to see those that are moving, and determine the direction of movement.

CHAPTER 4

An Overview of the Kola Military Bases

TOMAS RIES and JOHNNY SKORVE

Plate 4.1 shows an overall view of the Kola from space, providing a general overview of the Peninsula. The general location of military forces is shown on the accompanying Map 4.1. The locations marked with circles show the naval bases and naval aviation airfields, the locations marked with triangles show the Voyska PVO airfields and major SAM concentrations, while the shaded areas show the major ground forces concentrations. The naval and air bases are dealt with in more detail in Sections 6 and 7 and so will not be mentioned further at present. However the ground forces will be dealt with here. This is because it is difficult to examine their basing locations in more detail with the satellite resources at our disposal. In contrast to an airfield, naval base or other major installations, the ground forces are difficult to pick up because their military formations are composed of relatively small objects (people and vehicles) and their basing resources (housing and roads) are difficult to distinguish from civilian resources. Nonetheless by

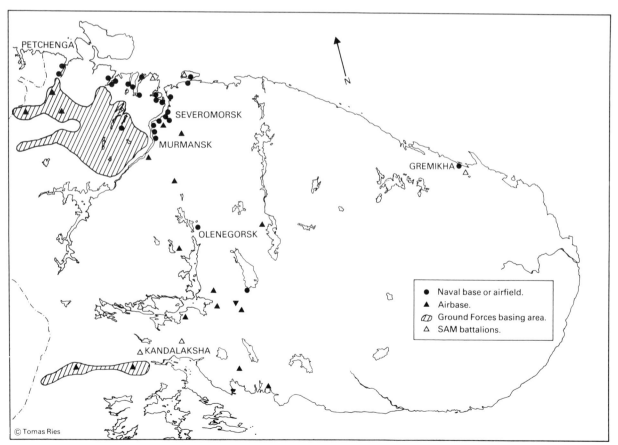

MAP 4.1. General outline of Kola military bases

47

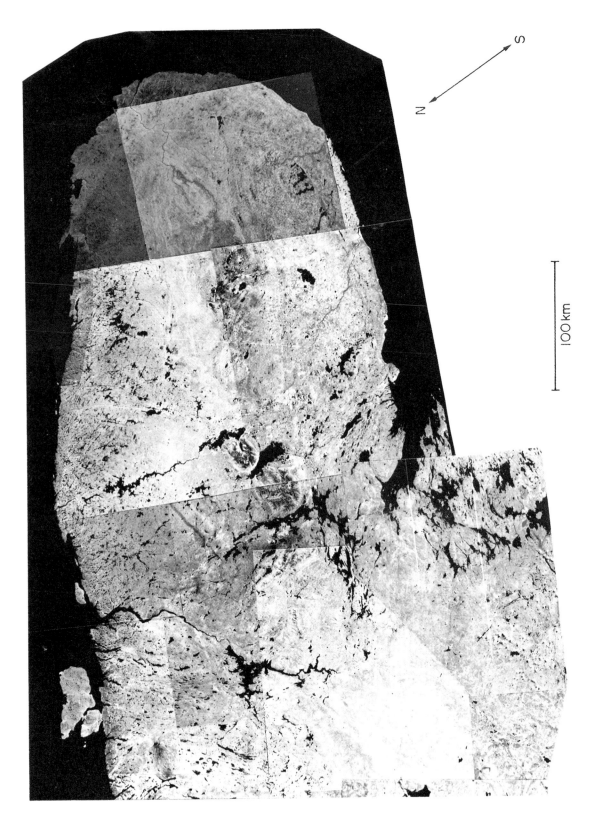

PLATE 4.1. General outline of Kola bases

combining the clues from open sources with a close examination of the satellite photos we have been able to obtain a general picture of the ground forces development in the northern Kola, facing Norway.

THE ARCTIC DETACHED FRONT FORCES ON THE KOLA.

Ground Forces.

There are two main peacetime concentrations of ground forces on the Kola, both probably part of the 6 Army, with its peacetime HQ in Petrozavodsk. The main force concentration lies between Murmansk and Petchenga, facing Norway, while a second concentration lies between Kandalaksha and Alakurtti. (See Map 4. 1.) These two areas are shown on the map. We shall deal briefly with each of these in turn.

The Murmansk–Petchenga ground forces are based in an area roughly one hundred kilometres long and eighty wide, between Murmansk and the Norwegian border. This area is outlined on Map 4.1. The satellite pictures show that there is a very dense road network here which is presently being expanded. This includes the building of a new, wide road over the last years in the area between Murmansk and Petchenga, linking the main east–west railway with one of the main basing complexes on the coast. *Landsat* MSS-5 imagery from 1980 shows that preparatory activities started at the southern end of lake Njalyaur. It is interesting that the new road started in the wilderness close to a small railroad station on the Murmansk–Petchenga/ Nikel line. A communications centre was built for handling cargo at this interchange between the railroad and the new road. By 1985 the *Landsat* pictures showed that the road construction was approaching the large naval basing area located in the eastern part of the fjord of Guba Zapadnaya Litsa, and it is expected that the road will be completed in 1986. The road has also led to the construction of additional facilities in the area. These are usually H-shaped offshoots of the road, appearing at regular intervals. They are probably military storage areas, possibly with accompanying helicopter landing pads. (See Plate 4.2.) It is important to note that in this area (north of the nickel mining complex) there appear to be no civilian activities at all. Thus the road work here is probably related either to the coastal naval bases along its northern edge, or with the ground forces in the area.

The actual combat units in this area consist of the following:[2]

45 Motorised Infantry Division (MRD)
129 Independent Arty Brigade
n.a. Air Assault Brigade
n.a. Air Assault Batallion
n.a. SS-1C *SCUD* B Brigade

In addition there are probably one mobilisable MRD and one air assault regiment available in the Murmansk area.

One should note that within the Soviet organisation of front forces both the SS-1C brigade and the artillery brigade are part of the Army level ORBAT,[3] and would therefore come directly under the command of the 6 Army HQ. There is at least one SS-1C brigade on the Kola. As these appear to be the only such formations in the NW TVD it indicates that the main focus of 6 Army operations would take place above the Arctic circle, and that this therefore is the main area of operations of the Arctic Detached Front.

There are reports that the two Air Assault Brigades have recently been expanded from regimental strength, and their equipment improved with the addition of air-droppable BMD-2 infantry fighting vehicles.[4]

The Kandalaksha–Alakurtti forces are located along the axis of the road and rail links crossing into northern Finland and include the following standing units:[5]

54 Motorised Infantry Division
n.a. Independent SAM Brigade

From their basing area it is roughly 400 kilometres to the Norwegian border at the strategic Skibotn entrance to the Troms defence concentrations. It is worth noting that it is virtually impossible for these standing forces to seriously contemplate a wartime crossing of Finland on their own. Such a venture would require a very considerable reinforcement and a massive injection of troops to secure the vulnerable logistic links rearwards. Finnish Lappland is characterised by extensive marshland, very heavy snow conditions for over half the year, great distances and a scarce road network. Because of their heavy mechanisation, and despite the advent of the helicopter, any major Soviet (and indeed Western) military force operating in Lappland is dependent upon the very scarce road network to advance and to remain supplied. Simply the destruction of the roads would considerably delay an invader. When this is combined with extensive mining the delay would increase further. If this is combined with extensive and co-ordinated guerilla operations along the entire depth of the enemy advance, mainly involving the further destruction and constant re-mining of the roads the delay would increase further, and the supplies reaching the fighting spearhead would diminish. Should this be combined with major counterattacks by the main Finnish forces, specially trained and equipped for the unique and very demanding nature of Lappland operations, with the most modern equipment, with very heavy firepower, and with full off-road mobility and the capacity to operate under all climatic conditions, the question of whether an invading force, even of several divisions, would at all be able to cross Finland becomes pertinent.

In addition it appears highly unlikely that either the Murmansk–Petchenga or Kandalaksha–Alakurtti force could commence offensive combat operations at short notice. These units are not in readiness Category A, though they have a relatively high Category B

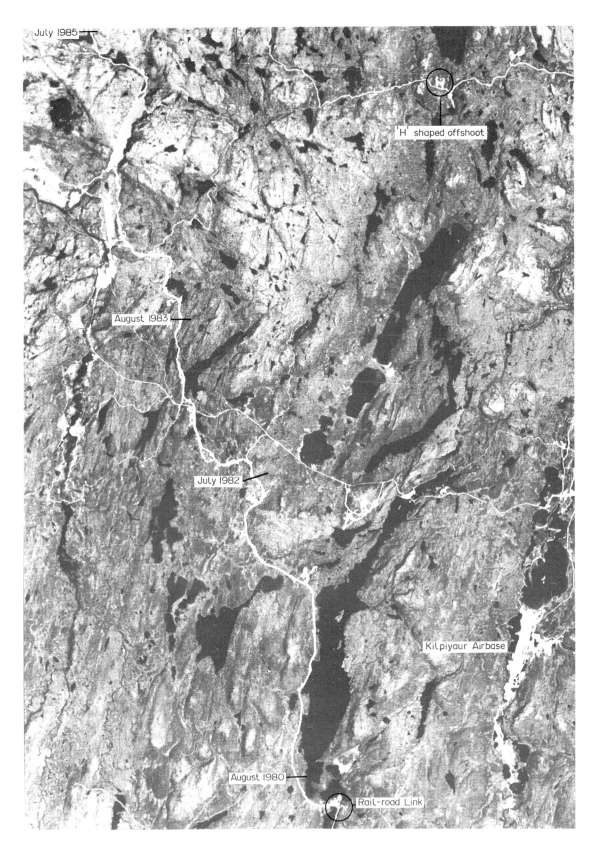

July 1985

'H' shaped offshoot

August 1983

July 1982

Kilpiyaur Airbase

August 1980

Rail-road Link

PLATE 4.2. The Road Network by Nyaljaur (Photo NASA)

ranking. Nor does the standing force, even if reinforced with the Murmansk mobilisable division, seem sufficient for a major offensive. They would therefore have to be reinforced by the further divisions of the 6 Army, located in the Leningrad region.

On the other hand both the 45 and 54 MRD have been specially equipped for Lappland operations (in the form of an increased complement of the more mobile and lighter MT-LB armoured fighting vehicles, and a slightly decreased number of the heavier and less mobile main battle tanks) and recently part of their old T-54/55 tanks have been replaced with T-72s. Their artillery regiments, as well as the 149 Independent Artillery Brigade, have also been modernised with self-propelled artillery. However while this does increase mobility to some extent it still does not permit major off-road operations in Lappland. Experience has shown that the MT-LB and the T-72 cannot cope adequately with the snow and marsh conditions north of the Arctic Circle. In addition it is worth noting that the off-road mobility of self-propelled artillery in Lappland snow and marsh conditions is very inferior to that of towed artillery.

One should also note that the modernisation of these ground forces is not an indication of a significant increase in the threat but is part and parcel of the armed forces. On the other hand the introduction of the airborne assault brigades with their new equipment is perhaps slightly more unusual. The same applies to the expansion and modernisation of the naval infantry brigades. (See below.)

Frontal Air Units.

The integral air units of the Arctic Detached Front consist of two main units: the Arctic Detached Front Frontal Aviation Army and the Army Aviation.

The Arctic Detached Front FA Army.

The Arctic Detached Front FA Army consists of about 175 aircraft. They are divided into one fighter ground attack (FGA) division and one detached tactical reconnaissance (recce) regiment:[6]

The Fighter Ground Attack Division.

1 regiment	50	MiG-21	*Fishbed*
1 regiment	50	MiG-27	*Flogger* D/J
1 regiment	50	Su-17	*Fitter* C/D

The Detached Tactical Reconnaissance Regiment

1 squadron	10	MiG-25	*Foxbat*
1 squadron	15	Su-17	*Fitter* H/K

The aircraft of the attack division of the Arctic Detached Front FA Army are not permanently based on the Kola in peacetime. Their main bases are located in the southern part of the Leningrad Military District, but they do rotate north regularly for exercises. In addition the airfield capacity on the Kola far exceeds the peacetime requirement, and during the

1970s extensive prepositioning of stocks for fighter aircraft was made, including Hardened Aircraft Shelters (HAS) and hardened fuel and ammunition depots. Some of these preparations are visible from the satellite photographs, such as the HAS, as well as the fact that in wintertime the runways are kept constantly cleared of snow. Thus the deployment of large FA forces to the Kola is actually a matter of hours, and the infrastructure is in place for sustained operations in the area. (See chapter 6.)

Permanently deployed on the Kola are the two squadrons of tactical recce aircraft. They are based at the top of the Kola panhandle,[7] probably at Salmiyaur airbase. (See Map 7.1.)

The Arctic Detached Front Army Aviation

The Army Aviation of the Arctic Detached Front is divided between Attack Helicopter (AH) units and transport helicopters and aircraft. They consist of:[8]

Attack and armed transport helicopter forces.

30	Mi-24	*Hind* D
40	Mi-8	*Hip* C/E
20	Mi-6	*Hook*

Transport aircraft and helicopters.

100	Mi-2	*Hoplite*
	Mi-8	*Hip* C
60	An-12	*Cub* and other smaller aircraft.

The organisation of these attack and transport helicopter units is shown on Table 4.1.

Of these forces a mixed complement of thirty attack and armed transport helicopters are based on the Kola, and about seventy transport helicopters.[9] However, once again the redeployment of the remainder of these forces northwards can take place very rapidly. It is worth noting that the introduction of this large helicopter force to the NW TVD is relatively recent, and is a cause for concern as it permits large scale tactical air assaults to take place. This increases the tempo and mobility of offensive operations on the tactical level. However, it does not mean that a large attacking force can do without resupply along roads, nor does it significantly alter the mobility of Soviet forces above the brigade level.

TABLE 4.1. Arctic Detached Front Army Aviation

Unit	No. Hel	Attached to
1 squadron	20	*Arctic Detached Front Command*
1 regiment	40	(Combined attack/transport regt)
1 squadron	10	(Special EW helicopter squadron)
1 squadron	20	*6 Army Command*
1 squadron	20	45 MRD (Murmansk-Petsamo)
1 squadron	20	54 MRD (Kandalaksha-Alakurtti)
1 squadron	20	*30 Army Corps*
1 squadron	20	36 Gd MRD (Pargolovo – south LMD)
1 squadron	20	*27 Army Corps*

The Assault Helicopter Regiment is probably under the direct command of the Arctic Detached Front HQ. This command also disposes of a special reduced helicopter squadron for electronic warfare on the Front level.

Amphibious Forces

In the event of war, the Arctic Detached Front probably has under its operational command the amphibious assault assets of the Northern Fleet, which would retain executive command of the operations of the amphibious assault vessels and other civilian transport ships which could be used. Naval infantry forces and other smaller associated units based on the Kola include:[10]

Petchenga	63 'Kirkenes' Naval Infantry Brigade
Petchenga area	n.a. Naval Spetsnaz Brigade

In addition there are indications that a new mobilisable naval infantry regiment has been established in Murmansk.

The 63 Naval Infantry Brigade has recently been enlarged from regimental size, as well as having much of its equipment modernised.[11] The older equipment has probably been allocated to the mobilisable regiment.

As one of the élite arms of the Soviet armed forces the 63 Naval Infantry Brigade is almost certainly in readiness Category A, and as such is operational in a very short time.

In addition one should note that the 45 MRD is probably specially trained for sea transport. This does not mean it could conduct an amphibious assault against a defended beach, nor that it could disembark without the help of port facilities. These are the tasks of the naval infantry. However it does mean that with the help of existing ro-ro tonnage on the Kola the 6 Army disposes of one division which could rapidly reinforce a secured harbour area captured by the naval infantry. This does away with some of the difficulties for a rapid advance across the ground, and would permit a larger scale *desant* operation in northern Norway. Always provided of course that the SLOC could be kept secure.

CHAPTER 5

Strategic Bases on the Kola

Map 5.1 shows the three main strategic bases on the Kola of importance to the GK SNF. As noted in Part I these include the SSBN forces and the intercontinental bomber forces.

THE ARCTIC SSBN FLOTILLA BASES

The circle indicates the main Arctic SSBN Flotilla base at Polyarnyy.

Polyarnyy: This is a main base for the *Delta*, *Yankee*, and *Hotel* III classes of SSBN. It is also the main arsenal for the Arctic SSBN Flotilla and the main submarine repair complex for the Northern Fleet. It contains a number of hardened submarine pens blasted into the fjord sides. (See Section 3 for details.)

In addition to this base the units of the Arctic SSBN Flotilla are also deployed in some of the other submarine bases of the Northern Fleet. These are described further in Section 6.

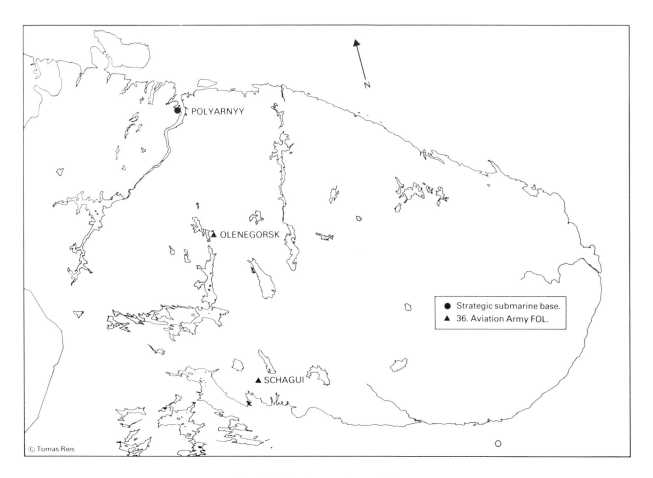

MAP 5.1. The three main strategic bases

THE 36 AVIATION ARMY AIRFIELDS.

The two triangles indicate the two main strategic bomber FOL at Olenegorsk and the possible new base constructed by the Schagui River.

Olenegorsk: This is actually a main operating base of the Northern Fleet Naval Aviation heavy long range aircraft. In addition it has been a major FOL for the naval aviation Tu-26 *Backfire* B of the Baltic Fleet, when these have deployed on the Kola for exercises. It has the longest existing runways on the Kola, with one main runway of 4,600 metres and a parallel secondary runway of 3,200 metres. It is also the main FOL of the 36 Aviation Army bombers when they deploy to the Kola for exercises, and has recently supported the operations of the latest version of the Tu-95, the *Bear* H, armed with the latest and only long range Soviet ALCM. The United States Department of Defense is also concerned by the fact that it could be used as a FOL for the theatre bomber forces of the 46 Aviation Army with its main base at Sol Tsy (between Leningrad and Pskov). Since it already contains the infrastructure for servicing the *Backfires* of the Naval Aviation it could also handle the modified *Backfires* of the Detached Aviation Armies. In combination with airborne refuelling (which one should note that Soviets do not appear to have fully mastered yet) it could give these *Backfires* the range to reach North America strategic targets.

Schagui: This base appears recently to have been enlarged. When completed it will have a main runway of equal length to that at Olenegorsk (4,600 metres) and will probably receive a second parallel runway. It is of course not certain, but appears likely to be destined as a 36 Aviation Army support airbase. The construction timing falls in well with the imminent deployment of the brand new *Blackjack* strategic intercontinental bomber. It could be that the decision has been made to construct a certain number of new strategic bomber airfields specially adapted for the new system.

Both these airfields are also discussed in Chapter 4.

CHAPTER 6

Naval Bases on the Kola

Map 6.1 and Plate 6.1 show the coastline between Petchenga and Ostrov Kil'din where the bulk of the Northern Fleet bases are located. Exceptions are the important new SSBN base at Gremikha and the possible submarine base at Umba, in the Bay of Kandalaksha. In addition the map and photo show some of the main Northern Fleet Naval Aviation Army airbases. The full complement of these on the Kola is depicted in Map 6.4 and Plate 7.1.

It is obvious that the Soviet Northern fleet really takes advantage of this stretch of ice-free fjords. To place the size of these bases in context, a comparison was made with the harbour facilities in Oslo, Norway's largest port. At Oslo the total pier length is 13,000 metres and it covers an area of 963,000 square metres. This shows that, for example, the naval ports

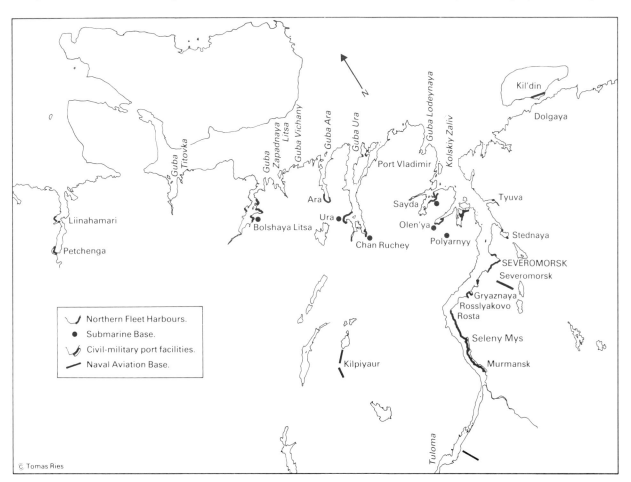

MAP 6.1. Northern Fleet Bases on the Kola

55

PLATE 6.1. Coastline between Ostrov Kil'din and Petchenga. (Photo NASA)

in one single fjord, Guba Zapadnaya Litsa, cover an area that is more than twice the size of Oslo harbour alone. Certain of these facilities are of course also for the civilian merchant fleet, notably for the Northern Fishing Fleet. However their main port area lies in Murmansk, with support facilities at Petchenga. Apart from these two locations all other major harbours on the Kola are highly restricted military bases, with no civilian access at all.

As noted earlier, the Northern Fleet is the largest and most modern of the four Soviet fleets. For a detailed examination of its present composition and the evolution of its force structure the reader is referred to the forthcoming study on this subject by John Kristen Skogan. Here we shall focus mainly on the basing infrastructure of this Fleet, with the exception of the Naval Aviation Forces, which will be outlined in some detail.

HEADQUARTERS AND MISCELLANEOUS INSTALLATIONS.

HQ Northern Fleet: Severomorsk.
The peacetime Headquarters of the Northern Fleet is located at Severomorsk.[12] This is also the main docking facility for large surface vessels including the *Kirov*, *Kiev*, and other major surface warships and amphibious vessels, and contains main Northern Fleet depot and storage areas, linked by rail to the southern part of the Leningrad Military District.

HQ Coastal Defence: Polyarnyy.
The Headquarters of the Coastal Defence for the Kola Peninsula is located at Polyarnyy,[13] which also is the main submarine base and repair complex on the Kola. (See below.)

Main Arsenals: Severomorsk, Stednaja, Polyarnyy.
There are three major Northern Fleet arsenals, located at Severomorsk, Stednaja and Polyarnyy.[14] A major weapons arsenal for the surface vessels is almost certainly located at Stednaja, and it is here that a large explosive fire in May 1984 destroyed between twenty-five and thirty per cent of the Northern Fleet's SAM stockpile and

surface-to-surface missiles.[15] The depot is situated eight kilometres north-east of the main naval base of Severomorsk, south of Guba Serednaya. Temporal studies of *Landsat* MSS-pictures show that this depot was new when it exploded. The first sign of preparatory work supporting the construction of the depot was seen on an MSS-picture taken in the summer of 1980. Roadwork had then started between Severomorsk and the site that later was to become the depot. *Landsat* pictures taken two years later show that the construction had entered an advanced stage with a new road completed between Severomorsk and the depot. Satellite pictures from 1983 give an impression that the construction was very nearly finished at that stage.

The main nuclear weapons arsenal for the submarine forces is probably located at Polyarnyy.

Main Repair Facilities:
Major repair facilities and naval dockyards on the Kola are located at Rosta[16]. The satellite pictures also show major facilities at Severomorsk, at Rosslyakovo (where the large 80,000 ton capacity dry dock purchased from Sweden in 1979 is sited) and along the length of the Murmansk waterfront.

The new dry dock at Rosslyakovo is visible on the *Landsat* images. It is 330 metres long and eighty-eight metres wide and arrived in the Murmansk fjord in 1980. It is capable of taking in vessels up to the *Kiev* size, and is the largest floating dry dock in the Soviet Union.

In addition special repair facilities for submarines are concentrated in the Polyarnyy submarine complex, including hardened wharves blasted into the cliffsides[17]. In 1974 the base received a heated, floating dry dock 100 metres long and of about 4,500 tons capacity. However this is too small to accomodate the *Delta* or *Yankee* class SSBNs though this is their main base. [18] However one should note that the main construction yards, including major repair facilities, are located beyond the Kola, at the '402' yard by Severodvinsk and the 'Krasnjaja-Kuznija' yards by Arkhangelsk.

SUBMARINE BASES.

There are at least seven major submarine bases on the northern coastline of the Kola. Of these, six are concentrated to the fjords between Murmansk and Poluostrov Rybachiy. The seventh, Gremikha, is located so far east that is outside this map. It is shown on Map 4.1.

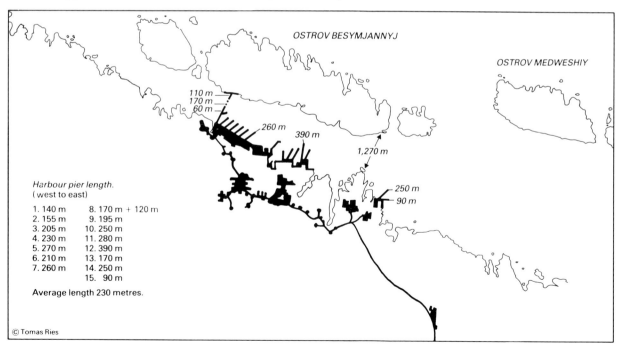

MAP 6.2. Gremikha Naval Base

Polyarnyy: Previously the main submarine base and peacetime headquarters of the Northern Fleet Submarine Flotilla lay in Polyarnyy.

Polyarnyy today remains a major Northern Fleet submarine base. It houses much of the SSBN Flotilla, and includes a large number of submarine bunkers blasted into the cliffsides.[19] In addition it houses some of the Northern Fleet SSGN, SSN, SSG and SS classes of submarine.[20] Finally, as noted earlier, it is the main Northern Fleet submarine repair and replenishment wharf.

Gremikha: This is a recently modernised and enlarged base probably built specially for the new large submarines appearing in the Soviet fleets, such as the *Oscar* class. This submarine is so large that earlier hardened installations could not accommodate it. The base is also interesting in that it is one of the few major naval installations located east of Ostrov Kil'din, lying some three hundred kilometres east of the Murmansk–Bolshaya Litsa basing concentrations. It is in fact located as far east as icing conditions permit, lying at the very edge of the winter ice limit. The base itself is very large and well protected. It lies between the shore and a long island, with the intervening channel filled with quays. The western end of the opening has been closed off partly by two piers, and the landward cliffsides appear to have been excavated and consist of hardened submarine bunkers. On the hillsides about one kilometre inland there are what appear to be radar sites, and it is possible that there are mobile SAM systems in the area.

On *Landsat* imagery taken in 1985 it was possible, for the first time, to observe the Gremikha base. With respect to the optimum advantage of the local topographical conditions. (See accompanying Map 6.2. and Photo 6.2.) To the east and north-east the base is sheltered by the long, sharp peninsula Cape Sswjatoi Nos. To the north and north-west, the Gremikha base is completely protected from the rough Barents Sea by the four kilometres long island Ostrov Besymjannyj, lying parallel to the coast. This forms a natural channel, 4,000 metres long and 600-800 metres wide, within which the port facilities of the base are located. The satellite images show that the harbour can be entered from both the east and the west. To the west, the entrance to the base is protected by two long jetties leaving a 170 metres wide 'gate' open to the base.

The main visible structure of the base is a 900 metres long pier with an extension toward the inside, forming a platform that is up to 200 metres wide, covering 150,000 square metres. From the pier, seven parallel jetty-like quays run in the direction 20 degrees north of east. The average length of these jetties is 210 metres. Inland 500-1000 metres from the port area there are buildings, installations and roads serving as a support system for the base.

Further to the east, the platform continues as a considerably narrower pier. From its eastern end, a new set of another eight jetties are spread eastward. Their average length is 240 metres. Here there are fewer buildings and constructions beyond the shoreline. From this area a road runs to the south leading to an area with more buildings and installations.

In addition to these two main submarine bases there are five further submarine basing complexes housing the SSGN, SSN, SSG and SS classes of submarine. Some of these also house elements of the Arctic SSBN Flotilla, such as the *Typhoon* and *Delta* classes.

Bolshaya Litsa:[21] This consists of four harbour areas, located inside the larger fjord of Guba Zapadnaya Litsa. They are mainly located along the eastern shores of Guba Zapadnaya Litsa with smaller facilities on the western side. This fjord has five pier systems with a total length of 20,600 metres, and the combined quay areas have been measured to be 2,770,000 m^2. (See Map 6.4. and Plate 6.3.)

Ura Guba and *Chan Ruchey*: The inlet of Guba Ura[22] contains two submarine bases, located at Ura and at Chan Ruchey. The Ura base area is connected to the western bay of Guba Ura by a wide road. At the innermost point of this latter bay there is a second naval port, with a 5,700 metres long pier system that covers an area of 530,000 square metres.

Sayda: The inlet of Guba Sayda contains one base at Sayda.[23] There has been a report that one of the four large underground SSBN tunnels under construction in the Soviet Union has been placed at Sayda.[24] This is unlikely as this is probably not an SSBN base. Should such a tunnel exist it is more likely to lie at Gremikha.

Guba Palo: The inlet of Guba Palo contains one submarine base at Olenya.[25]

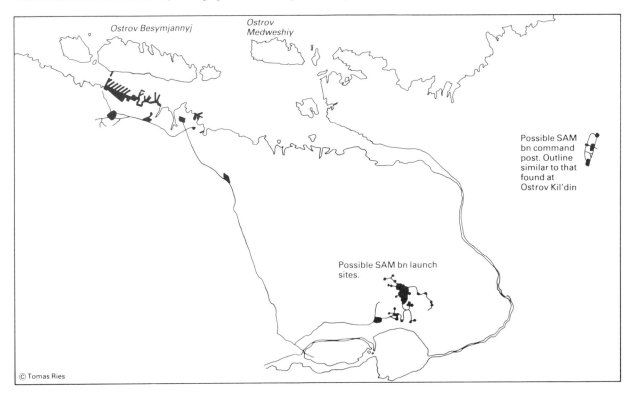

MAP 6.3. Gremikha and Surroundings

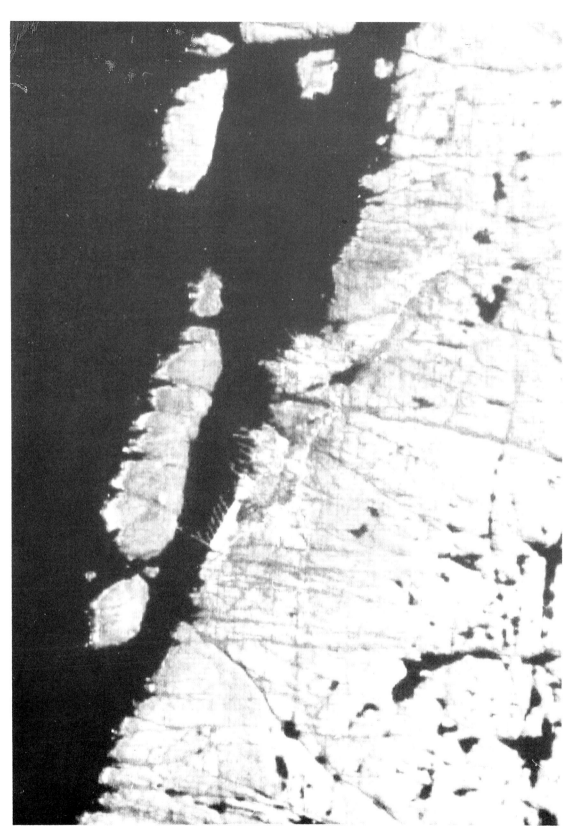

PLATE 6.2. Gremikha Naval Base. (Photo NASA)

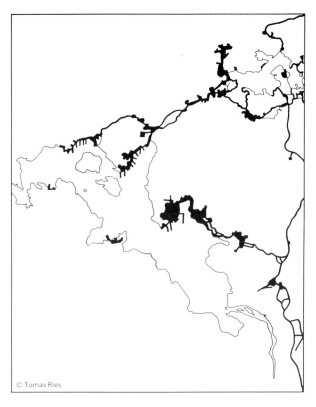

MAP 6.4. Bolshaya Litsa Submarine Bases

These aircraft operate from seven main airbases on the Kola employed by the Naval Aviation of the Northern Fleet. In addition they operate one airfield located next to Arkhangelsk and one airfield on southern Novaya Zemlya. Of the seven Kola airbases only five are shown on Map 6.1 as the remaining two (Olenegorsk and Umbozero) lie below the southern edge of this map. However all of these bases are also shown on Map 7.1. The seven bases are:

Severomorsk,[27] with a runway of 3,100 metres.

Olenegorsk,[28] with a main runway of 4,600 metres, and a parallel runway of 3,200 metres. This is the main FOL of the Tu-26 *Backfire* B medium/long range naval attack aircraft and anti-shipping aircraft. These aircraft are not permanently based on the Kola, but when they have deployed here from the Baltic for exercises they have used this base.[29] This is also the home base of one Regiment of Tu-95 *Bear* D long-range recce aircraft.[30] This is also the FOL used so far by the strategic intercontinental bombers of the 36 Aviation Army when they have deployed north for exercises.

Kilpiyaur,[31] with three runways. The main runway is 3,640 metres long with a parallel runway of 2,500 metres. The third strip is slightly to the south of the two main strips and is 1,860 metres.

Umbozero,[32] main runway 3,300 metres, parallel runway 2,800 metres.

Kil'din,[33] with a main runway of 2,600 metres and a parallel runway of 1,250 metres. (See Map 6.5. and Photo 6.4.)

Murmansk NE,[34] with a runway of 2,050 metres.

Gryaznaya,[35] which is a seaplane base and home base of the Be-12 *Mail* ASW flying boats.

NAVAL AVIATION

The Naval Aviation of the Northern Fleet is the equivalent of one Air Army, and is composed of one division of anti-shipping aircraft, one regiment of recce aircraft, one regiment of ASW aircraft, one regiment of ASW helicopters split into smaller units, one regiment of transport aircraft, and one squadron of fighter attack aircraft. These forces are shown in Table 6.1.:[26]

SURFACE FORCES

There are nine main bases on the Kola for the Northern Fleet surface vessels, of which Murmansk is a mixed civilian-military facility also serving the Barents Fishing Fleet and merchant ships. These bases are all concentrated to the fjords between Petsamo and Ostrov Kil'din. As for the submarine bases, they present a concentrated and vulnerable target.

TABLE 6.1. Northern Fleet Naval Aviation Organisation

Anti-shipping	1 regiment	3 squadron	65	Tu-16 *Badger* C
	1 regiment	3 squadron	65	Tu-16 *Badger* C
	1 regiment	3 squadron	65	Tu-16 *Badger* C
		1 squadron	15	Tankers
EW		1 squadron	5	An-12 *Cub* B
Recce	1 regiment	1 squadron	20	Tu-16 *Badger* D/F/K
		1 squadron	15	Tu-16 *Badger* H/J
		1 squadron	20	Tu-95 *Bear* D
ASW	1 regiment	2 squadron	40	Il-38 *May* Be-12 *Mail*
		2 squadron	35	Tu-95 *Bear* F
ASW Helicopters	1 regiment	1 squadron	20	Mi-4 *Haze* A
		1 squadron	25	Ka-27 *Helix*
		1 squadron	25	Ka-25 *Hormone*
Transport	1 regiment	3 squadron	70	Various
Fighter-attack	1 regiment	2 squadron	30	Yak-36 *Forger*

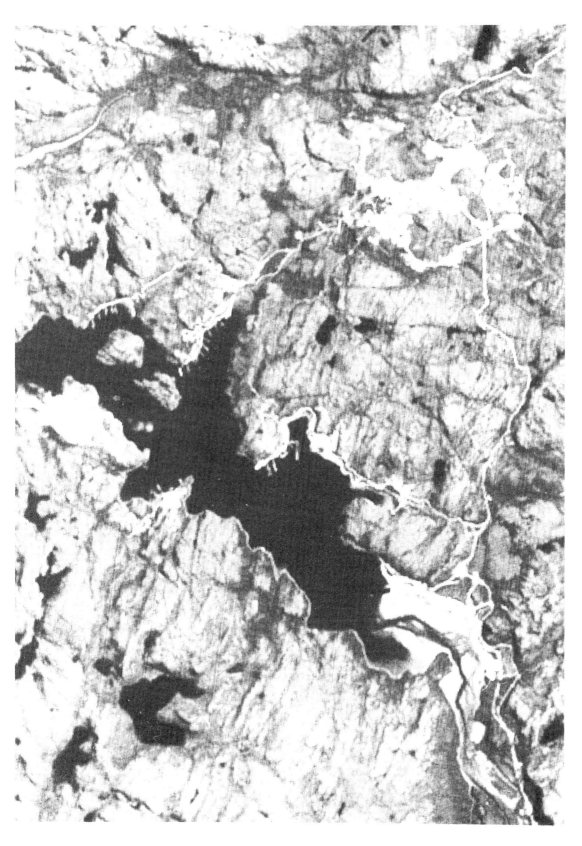

PLATE 6.3. Guba Zapadnaya Litsa Fjord. (Photo NASA)

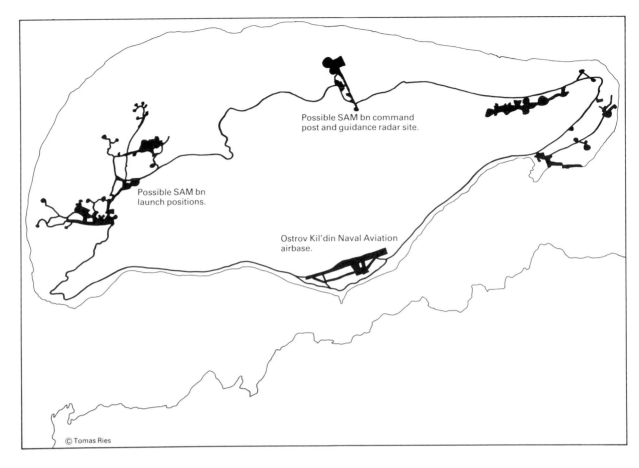

Possible SAM bn command
post and guidance radar site.

Possible SAM bn
launch positions.

Ostrov Kil'din Naval Aviation
airbase.

© Tomas Ries

MAP 6.5. Ostrov Kil'din Naval Aviation Base and SAM concentration

Severomorsk: The main base for surface vessels is located at Severomorsk, which handles the largest Northern Fleet vessels. These include the *Kirov* CGN, *Kiev* CVSG, *Kresta* II CG, *Slava* CG, *Sverdlov* CLC, *Sovremenny* DDG and *Udaloy* DDG. It can also handle a number of smaller vessels as well as large amphibious assault vessels of the *Ivan Rogov* class.

Ara: A second base for major surface vessels lies at Ara in the Guba Ara.[36] This handles ships up to cruiser size. The whole southern part of Guba Ara consists of an elongated, continuous line of piers forming a semicircle at the bottom of the fjord. Perpendicular to the shoreline are a considerable number of jetties. The piers at Ara have a total length of 5400 metres and cover an area of 780,000 square metres.

Tuva: This base handles the larger amphibious assault vessels[37].

Port Vladimir, Rosslyakovo, Dolgaya: These harbours handle a variety of smaller surface vessels.[38]

Liinaharmari, Petchenga: In addition smaller support bases have been constructed at Liinaharmari and Petchenga,[39] which probably serve both the amphibious assault forces and smaller strike forces of the Northern Fleet, such as *Nanuchka* class PG.

Murmansk: The very large harbour complex at Murmansk is a mixed civilian-military facility which, for the Northern Fleet, is mainly employed for repair work and training.[40]

The Murmansk harbour area has undergone a fairly constant development. When comparing *Landsat* MSS-pictures taken in 1973 and 1978, it became apparent that during this period a new, wide road had been built and completed. It connects the western side of the fjord opposite Murmansk with Polyarnyy and leads towards the other naval bases on the north-western side of the fjord. *Landsat* MSS-imagery also shows that some major changes took place in the Murmansk fjord from 1979-80. In 1979, construction started on the western side of the fjord. In 1982 it proved to be a new pier platform that has a rectangular form, measuring 380 × 250 metres. In 1980 construction started in the southern harbour of Murmansk, and about two years later a similar pier unit measuring 460 × 370 metres was ready.

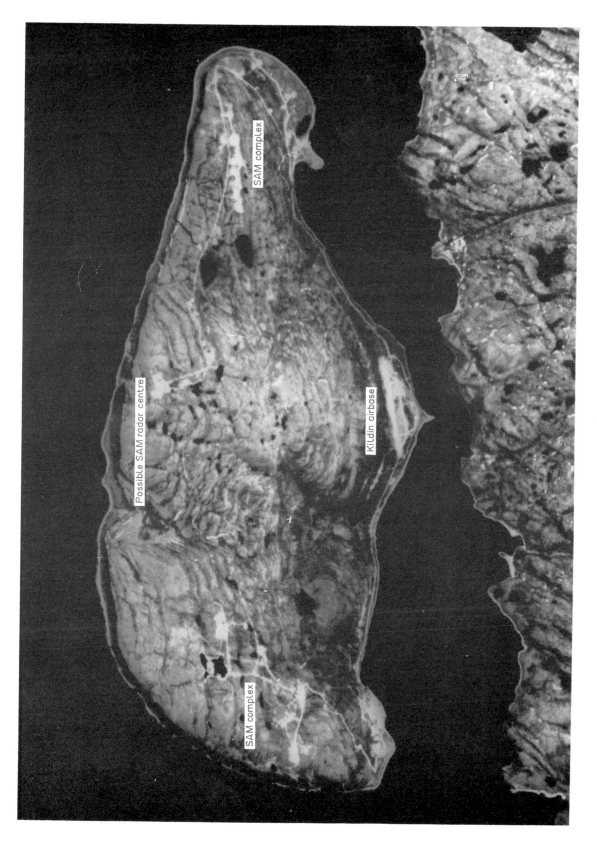

SAM complex

Possible SAM radar centre

Kildin airbase

SAM complex

PLATE 6.4. Ostrov Kil'din. (Photo NASA)

CHAPTER 7

Air Bases on the Kola

Map 7.1 shows the twenty-two most important airfields on the Kola Peninsula. These include six airfields operated and used by the Naval Aviation of the Northern Fleet, and one (Salmiyaur) which is the base of the two tactical recce squadrons based on the Kola of the Arctic Detached Front FA Army. In addition there are about eighteen further small dirtstrips of less than 800 metres scattered throughout the vast peninsula. But the airfields shown are those which can be used by fighter aircraft and other larger aircraft. Since the six main naval aviation bases already have been covered in Chapter 6 we shall not discuss them here, but they are shown on the map.

The remaining sixteen main airfields are administered by the HQ Arkhangelsk Air Defence Sector (AADS) of the Vojska PVO, which is responsible for their upkeep and readiness. This means that all the main airfields' runways and taxiways are kept permanently cleared of snow in winter, and full stocks of fuel, ammunition, spare parts and so forth, kept in readiness. During the 1970s a large programme for the prepositioning of stocks on the Kola airfields, as well as the construction of very many Hardened Aircraft Shelters, was completed.[41] It is estimated that this would permit a total force of about five hundred aircraft[42] to be based on and to operate permanently from the Kola bases in wartime. In addition, further aircraft could use the bases for refuelling.

As noted earlier, the only fighter aircraft permanently based on the Kola in peacetime are those of the IAPVO regiments of the Arkhangelsk ADS, with the exception of the two squadrons of recce fighters of the Arctic Detached Front FA Army. However, as has also been noted, fighter squadrons from the Arctic Detached Front FA Army and intercontinental strategic bombers from the 36 Aviation Army regularly deploy to the Kola for training exercises. Since 1985 this last force has included the most modern Soviet aircraft of this type presently operational, namely the Tu-95 *Bear* H equipped with the new AS-15 ALCM, which regularly operates on the Kola.[43] In addition, and far more alarming for the Nordic regional military

equilibrium, are the indications that detachments of Su-24 *Fencer* theatre nuclear/conventional bombers from the 24 Aviation Army at Chernyakhovsk in the Baltic have made preparations for wartime operations from certain of the Kola airfields.[44]

The IAPVO interceptor forces of the AADS which are permanently based on the Kola airfields include about one hundred interceptors out of a total force of 276 in the AADS. In addition there are six Airborne Early Warning (AEW) aircraft operating from this sector.[45] Since redeployment of forces is very fast, and the airfield capacity on the Kola is capable of handling almost twice as many aircraft as the Arkangelsk ADS IAPVO Divisions contain, the force of permanently based aircraft on the Kola could be increased very rapidly, or the force composition varied.

The total AADS IAPVO force of 276 interceptors is organised into two Fighter Air Defence Divisions, each probably part of one Air Defence Army (which includes SAM and radar forces). Each of the interceptor divisions consists of about one hundred aircraft organised into three regiments (each of some twenty-eight aircraft – including three squadrons of eight aircraft each, plus one command flight of four aircraft) and one command flight (four aircraft). In addition, there are two detached squadrons (each of about twelve aircraft) of older long range Arctic interceptors. Of this force, one division (or some one hundred interceptors) is permanently based on the Kola in peacetime.

The present Arkhangelsk Air Defence Sector (AADS) order-of-battle (ORBAT) is shown on Table 7.1.[46]

TABLE 7.1. Arkhangelsk Air Defence Sector
IAPVO ORBAT

Interceptors	3 regiment	75	MiG-23 *Flogger* B
	1 regiment	28	MiG-25 *Foxbat* A
	2 regiment	48	MiG-31 *Foxhound*
	3 regiment	75	Su-15 *Flagon* E/F
	1 regiment	ca 20	Yak-28P *Firebar*
	1 regiment	ca 20	Tu-28P *Fiddler*
AEW	1 squadron	6	Tu-126 *Moss*

There are also reports that the first MiG-29 *Fulcrum* have now begun deploying to Kola bases.

64

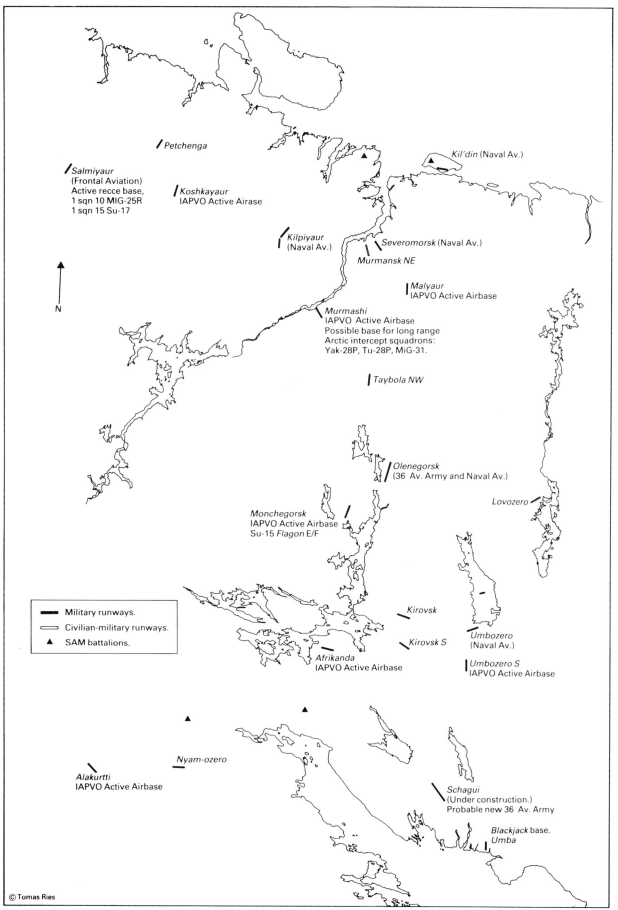

/ *Petchenga*

Kil'din (Naval Av.) ▲

/ *Salmiyaur*
(Frontal Aviation)
Active recce base,
1 sqn 10 MIG-25R
1 sqn 15 Su-17

/ *Koshkayaur*
IAPVO Active Airase

↑

N

/ *Kilpiyaur*
(Naval Av.)

/ *Severomorsk* (Naval Av.)

Murmansk NE

/ *Malyaur*
IAPVO Active Airbase

/ *Murmashi*
IAPVO Active Airbase
Possible base for long range
Arctic intercept squadrons:
Yak-28P, Tu-28P, MiG-31.

/ *Taybola NW*

/ *Olenegorsk*
(36 Av. Army and Naval Av.)

Lovozero /

Monchegorsk
IAPVO Active Airbase
Su-15 *Flagon* E/F

▬	Military runways.
□	Civilian-military runways.
▲	SAM battalions.

/ *Kirovsk*

/ *Umbozero*
(Naval Av.)

/ *Kirovsk S*

/ *Umbozero S*
IAPVO Active Airbase

Afrikanda
IAPVO Active Airbase

▲

▲

\ *Alakurtti*
IAPVO Active Airbase

\ *Nyam-ozero*

\ *Schagui*
(Under construction.)
Probable new 36 Av. Army

Blackjack base.
Umba

© Tomas Ries

MAP 7.1. Air Bases on the Kola

PLATE 7.1. The Central Kola Main Airbase Area. (Photo NASA)

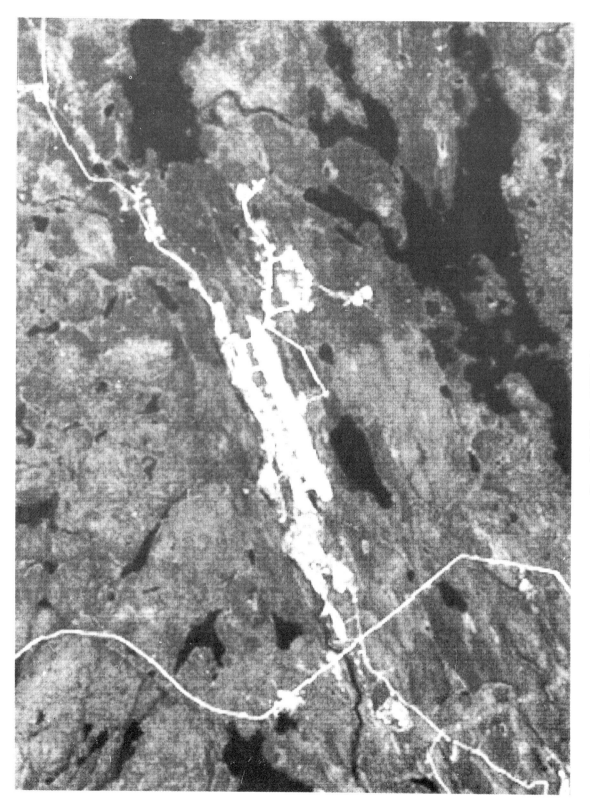

PLATE 7.2. Malyaur IAPVO Airbase

PLATE 7.3. Schagui Airbase Under Construction

The Tu-126 *Moss* are presently being replaced by the more modern and capable Il-76 *Mainstay* AWACS, and the old Yak-28P *Firebar* and Tu-28P *Fiddler* are probably in the process of being phased out in favour of the MiG-31 *Foxhound*. In addition it appears that the Mig-29 *Fulcrum* is presently being deployed on the Kola.

Eight of the sixteen airfields on the Kola kept in constant readiness are the peacetime operating bases[47] of the Kola Interceptor Division of the AADS. They are:

Salmiyaur, main runway 3,000 metres, secondary runway 1,250 metres.

Koshkayaur, 3,800 metre runway.

Murmashi, 4,200 metre runway.

Malyaur. As an example of the Kola airfields Malyaur is described here in greater detail. (See Photo 7.2.) The main runway is aligned in the north-south direction and is 2,550 metres long and seventy-five metres wide. About ninety metres to the east is a taxi track that runs parallel to the main track, and it is twenty-five metres wide. Further to the east another taxi track, also twenty-five metres wide, leads to a row of protected aircraft shelters. To the north of this area there is a group of buildings close to the main road eastward from Murmansk. To the southwest of the main runway, there is a large complex of protective airplane shelters. There are two types of shelters, the majority of them measure 60 × 100 metres each, while the smaller ones are about half of that size. There are about twenty airplane shelters of the large type in the Malyaur area.

Monchegorsk, 3,100 metre runway. Base for Su-15 *Flagon* E/F.

Afrikanda, 3,200 metre runway.

Umbozero S, 3,850 metre main runway, 3,000 metre secondary runway.

Alakurtti, runway length not available.

The remaining eight reserve airbases are kept at a constant state of readiness but are not in regular peacetime use, though they are employed for exercises. They are:

Petsamo, 2,000 metre runway.

Taybola NW, 2,500 metre runway.

Lovozero, 700 metre main runway, 400 metre second strip.

Kirovsk, 2,400 metre runway.

Kirovsk S, 3,400 metre main runway, 2,500 metre secondary runway.

Nyam-Ozero, runway length not available.

Umba, 1,300 metre runway.

Schagui, 4,600 metre runway presently under construction. (See Photo 7.3.) Schagui will probably become a main airbase when completed.

Landsat pictures taken during the summer of 1985 revealed that a new, large military airbase was being built next to the river Schagui, thirty-five kilometres west-north-west of the town of Umba and its older and much smaller airfield. The construction was at that time at an advanced stage. The new airbase construction area involves a strip approximately 4,600 metres long and 500 metres wide. The total construction area measures 3.3 × 8.2 kilometres. The length of the runway is very similar to that of the airbase for strategic bombers at Olenegorsk, indicating, along with the general development of the Soviet long range strategic nuclear bomber forces, that probably this new one will be another airbase for strategic bombers.

This list does not include the airfield Murmansk NE, which is, however, shown on the map. This is because this airport is a dual civil-military facility. However, in wartime it is, of course, clear that it would also play a military role.

Finally, the main SAM concentrations of the AADS ZRT are shown on Map 7.1. These forces consist of about seventy fixed missile complexes equipped with the ageing SA-2 *Guideline*, the modernised SA-3 *Goa Grumble*.[48] Their Kola organisation probably consists of two Rocket Regiments (each of three to five Launch Battalions) and one to two Detached Launch Battalions. Each launch battalion employs between six to eight launchers.

One of the two Rocket Regiments is stationed so that it covers the approaches to the Murmansk inlet. There are SAM positions on Ostrov Kil'din and on the heights between Port Vladimir and Toros Ostrov. In addition there are almost certainly further detachments on the heights overlooking the main naval bases west from Murmansk inlet, and possibly also at key airfields or industrial targets. The second Rocket Regiment is probably located at two points in the vicinity of Kandalaksha in the southern part of the Kola peninsula.[49] Finally one or two detached battalions may operate separately in remote areas, such as at Gremikha.

REFERENCES

1. For some references to satellite reconnaissance see:

    Aviation Week and Space Technology, 6 October 1980.

    KLASS, Philip: *Secret Sentries in Space*, Random House, 1st. ed., 1971. Chapters 15 and 17.

    NASA Authorisation, Fiscal Year 1974. Washington, D.C., Senate Committee on Aeronautical and Space Sciences, 1973.

    FRANZ HANS–JOCHIM '*Physique Geographie der Soviet Union*'.

    SKORVE '*The use of Low Solar Angle Orbital Imagery in the Study of Solid Planetary and Lunar Surfaces*', Memorie della Societa Astronomica Italiana, 1981.

2. *Militaerbalansen 1985-1986*. Oslo, Den Norske Atlanterhavskomitén, 1986: p. 130-131.

RIES, Tomas: 'Defending the Far North.' *International Defense Review*, Vol. 17, No. 7, 1984: pp. 873-880.

VEGO, Dr. Milan: 'Streitkräfte des Wartschauer Paktes im baltischen Raum.' *Osterreichische Militärische Zeitschrift*, XXIV. Jahrgang, Nr. 1, 1986: pp. 32-36

3. *The Military Balance 1985-1986*. London, IISS, 1985: p. 187.
4. *International Defense Review*, Vol. 19, No. 1, January 1986: p.14.
5. *Militaerbalansen*, op. cit., p. 130-131.
6. *Militaerbalansen 1985-1986*. Oslo, Den Norske Atlanterhavskomité, 1986: p. 132.
7. HOLST, Johan Jørgen: 'Norway's Search for a Nordpolitik.' *Foreign Affairs*, Vol. 60, No. 1, Fall 1981: p. 71.
8. *Militaerbalansen*, op. cit., p. 132.
9. *Militaerbalansen*, op. cit., p. 132.
10. *Militaerbalansen*, op. cit., p. 131.

11. RIES: 'Defending . . .', op. cit., p. 875.

12. KRISTENSEN, Helge: 'Truslen fra Kola – Sovjets strategiske base 2,000 km fra Danmark.' *Berlingske Weekendavisen*, 24/30 Juli, 1981: 13.

    VEGO: 'Streitkräfte . . .', op. cit., p. 129.

13. KRISTENSEN: 'Truslen fra . . .', op. cit., p. 13.

14. 'Sowjetische Schiffswerfte.' *Osterreichische Militärische Zeitschrift*, XXIII. Jahrgang, Heft 2, 1985: p. 129.

15. *International Herald Tribune*, 23/4 June 1984.
    International Herald Tribune, 25 June, 1984.
    'Munitionsexplosion bei der Nordflotte.' *Osterreichische Militärische Zeitschrift*, XXII. Jahrgang, Heft 5, 1984: p. 470.

16. 'Sowjtetische . . .', op. cit., p. 129.

17. VEGO, Dr. Milan: 'Die sowjetischen Streitkräfte in Nordeuropa.' *Osterreichische Militärische Zeitschrift*, Jahrgang XXIII., Heft 6, 1985: p. 535-6.

18. 'Die Nordflotte der sowjetischen Kriegsmarine.' *Osterreichische Militärische Zeitschrift*, Heft 1, 1978: 41.

19. VEGO: 'Die sowjetiscshen . . .', op. cit., p. 535-6.

20. ibid., p. 535-6.

21. ARKIN and FIELDHOUSE: *Nuclear* . . ., op. cit., pp. 252-263.

    KRISTENSEN: 'Truslen fra . . .', op. cit., p. 13.

    VEGO: 'Die sowjetischen . . .', op. cit., p. 535-6.

22. KRISTENSEN: 'Truslen fra . . .', op. cit., p. 13.

    VEGO: 'Die sowjetischen . . .', op. cit., p. 535-6.

23. ARKIN and FIELDHOUSE: *Nuclear* . . ., op. cit., pp. 525-563.

    KRISTENSEN: 'Truslen fra . . .', op. cit., p. 13.

24. *Washington Times*, 27 March, 1984: p. 1.

25. ARKIN and FIELDHOUSE: *Nuclear* . . ., op. cit., p. 252-263.

    KRISTENSEN: 'Truslen fra . . .', op. cit., p. 13.

    VEGO: 'Die sowjetischen . . .', op. cit., p. 252-6.

26. *Militaerbalansen 1985-1986*, op. cit., p. 131.

27. VEGO: 'Die sowjetischen . . .', op. cit., p. 533-4.

28. ibid., p. 533-4.

29. *Soviet Military Power 1983*. Washington D.C., Department of Defense, 2nd. rev. ed., 1983: p. 25.

30. ARKIN and FIELDHOUSE: *Nuclear* . . ., op. cit., pp. 252-263.

31. ibid., p. 533-4.

32. ibid., p. 533-4.

33. ibid., p. 533-4.

34. ibid., p. 533-4.

35. 'Severomorsk.' *Joint Operations Graphic (Ground)*, St. Louis, Missouri, Aeronautical Chart and Information Center, US Air Force, Series 1501 / Sheet Nr. 35, 36-9 / Edition 1, Scale 1:250,000, 1971.

36. KRISTENSEN: 'Truselen fra . . .', op. cit., p. 13.

37. ibid., p. 13.

38. ibid., p. 13.

39. VEGO: 'Die sowjetischen . . .', op. cit., p. 535-6.

40. 'Die Nordflotte . . .', op. cit., p. 41.

41. *Kungliga Krigsvetenskapsakademiens Handlingar och Tidskrift*, Nr. 2, 1985: s. 81-83.

42. VEGO: 'Die sowjetischen . . .', op. cit., p. 535.

43. *Flight International*, 18 May, 1985: p. 33.

44. *Flight International*, 18 May, 1985: pp. 32-33.

45. *Militaerbalansen 1985-1986*, op. cit., p. 132.

46. *Militaerbalansen 1985-1986*, op. cit., p. 132.

47. RIES: 'The Defense of . . .', op. cit., p. 875.

48. *Militaerbalansen 1985-1986*, op. cit., p. 132.

49. KRISTENSEN: 'Truselen fra . . .', op. cit., p. 13.

CHAPTER 8

The Economic Geography of the Kola Peninsula

JOHNNY SKORVE

The Soviet Union is divided into fifteen Socialist Republics which are based on the fifteen most populous and advanced nationality groups in the country. The republics are divided into administrative provinces called *oblast*. The *oblast* is a unit without any nationality overtones.

The Kola Peninsula belongs to the Murmansk *oblast* with its centre located in Murmansk. The Murmansk *oblast* belongs to the Leningrad Economic Region.

There are no updated statistics available on the Murmansk *oblast*. However it is obvious that this is a very expansive part of the Soviet Union. In 1971 the total population of the Murmansk *oblast* was 815,000. With an area of 144,900 square kilometres, the population density was 5.6 per square kilometre. However, in actual fact 89 per cent are concentrated in the military bases or in urban areas adjacent to major industries, leaving most of the Murmansk *oblast* virtually unpopulated. By 1979 the total population of the Murmansk *oblast* had grown to 965,000, with 381,000 concentrated in the Murmansk area.

For the last thirty years a major cause of this population build-up on the Kola has been due to the massive military investments in the area. However, the economic resources in and around the Kola Peninsula have also played a part in this development. The Kola is rich in natural resources like iron, nickel, copper and other important metals and minerals, and the Murmansk based Atlantic fishing fleet is one of the main single suppliers of protein in the USSR.

THE METAL AND MINERAL RESOURCES.

The nickel deposits are one of the main mineral resources of the Kola. They are located in the regions of Petchenga (prior to World War II the Finnish port of Petsamo), Allerechen, Monchegorsk and Lovnoozersk. At these four locations copper is also found, as is the case in the Imandra-Varzugd area. The Petchenga ore field with more than twenty copper-nickel deposits is an up to 35 kilometres wide and 60 kilometres long formation extending north-westward. In addition to these copper-nickel mixed ores, there are 110 pure nickel intrusions within the Petchenga formation. The mining here has been going on for a long time, and thus also during the time when this was Finnish territory until the end of World War II.

After 1945 the search for new natural resources, and the mapping and testing of those found, became an important goal in the post-war development of the Soviet Union. On the Kola Peninsula this resulted in the start of mining activities at Olenegorsk in 1954. From this open cast mine, which is one of the largest Soviet iron mines, iron concentrates are produced from ferruginous quartzite.

The start of the Olenegorsk mining was timed with the starting up in 1955 of the large iron and steel plant at Cherepovets, east of Leningrad and more than one thousand kilometres south of Olenegorsk. Larger volumes of iron concentrates were produced when mining started in the Eno-Kovdor area with the same type of iron deposits. In 1974 the Olenegorsk-Kovdor mines supplied the Cherepovets plant with ten million tons of iron concentrates. The total reserves in these mines have been estimated to one point two billion tons.

The alkaline rocks of the Khibin Massif in the central part of the Kola peninsula contain an enormous amount of nepheline. This serves as raw material for the extraction of aluminium. The production of alumina (aluminium oxide), with the industrial method involved, in turn provides by-products like potash, calcinated soda and high grade cement. The

Kola nepheline contains 20 to 30 per cent alumina, and the production of nepheline in 1974 gave 400,000 tons of alumina, or about 10 per cent of the total production in the Soviet Union.

The Khibinian Massif also contains a large volume of apatite. This is an acid phosphatic salt of calcium and it also contains fluorides. Apatite is valuable in the production of fertilizers and in particular of super-phosphate.

Geologically apatite occurs here as large lenses, the most important ones being up to 4 kilometres long with a thickness up to 200 metres. The mining takes place at the south central foot of the Khibinian Massif close to Kirovsk, the town that was built when apatite mining started. In 1975, fifteen million tons of Kirovsk apatite was produced. The apatite formation here is enormous, more than 2 billion tons. This exceeds the combined apatite resources of the whole Western world by a factor of two and a half.

Important minerals like feldspar, mica and quartz are found near the shores of the White Sea, and also in the region of the Chupinskion fjord to the south of Kandalaksha. In the central part of the Kola Penin-sula, near Lovozero, rocks contain tantalum, an im-portant non-ferrous light metal.

THE FISHERY RESOURCES

The Atlantic fishing fleet based in the Murmansk area ranks first after overtaking the Far East and the Caspian as the Soviet Union's chief catcher of fish. Cod, the most attractive and important species, is concentrated in an area including the coastal zone of northern Norway and across the southern part of the Barents Sea to the Novaya Zemlya Ridge. However, the activity of the large fishing fleet is not restricted to local waters. It has been expanded continuously, and regular fishing also takes place in the waters of the Norwegian Sea, around Iceland, in the North Atlantic, and off Greenland and Newfoundland. In addition to cod, the Murmansk fleet catch yields haddock, sea perch, herring and other sorts of fish. The expansion of the fleet, combined with more modern equipment and methods, has resulted in an increased volume of fish catch. In 1970 the Murmansk fleet caught 235 per cent more fish than in 1960, and the fish catch in 1970 was more than ten times the 1950 volume.

ENERGY REQUIREMENTS AND PRODUCTION.

Up to the 1960s the Murmansk *oblast* had many small hydro-electrical power plants using steep rivers. These provided most of the electricity needed in the

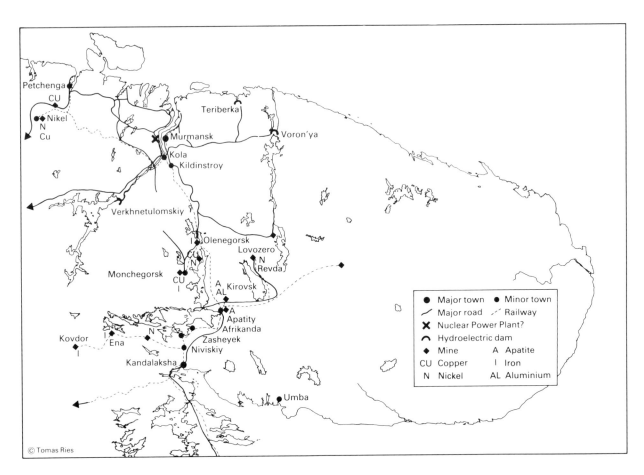

MAP 8.1. The Economic Infrastructure of the Kola

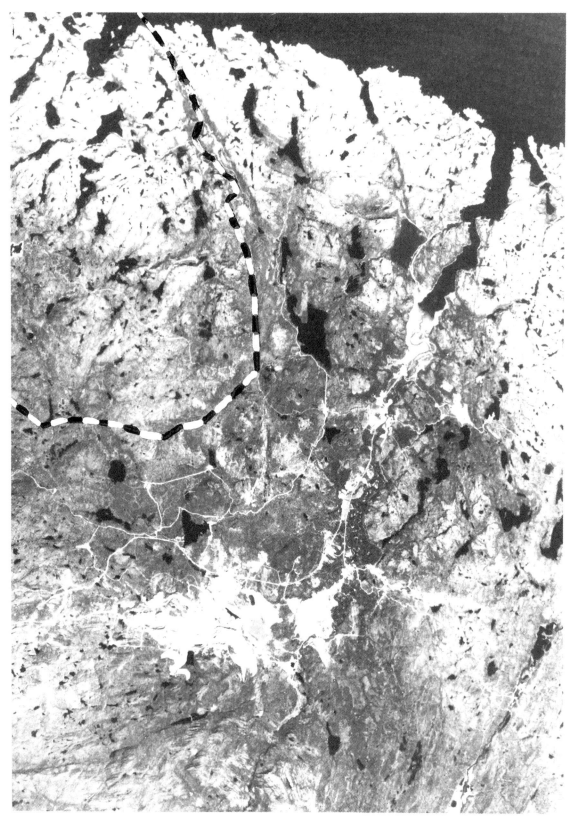

PLATE 8.1. Landsat Thematic Mapper picture from August 1st 1985 of the Petchenga area. In the upper left of this 21 × 30 kilometre section a part of north-east Norway is seen and also in the upper left the Petchenga fjord. The lower half is dominated by the very extensive nickel copper mining complex. (Photo NASA)

area. However, the combined large expansion of industrial activity and the strong military build-up on Kola sharply increased the demand for more electrical power. As a result several rather large hydro-electrical power plants were constructed by building dams creating artificial lakes like Ozero Notozero and Ozero Kevlyaksh'yavr. Recently this hydro-electric grid has been expanded by the construction of a new large water power dam south of Teriberka, with the reservoir filled with water for the first time during the summer of 1985. These hydro-electric constructions were discovered on *Landsat* images during the Kola study.

In addition the Murmansk *oblast* energy requirements have been met through nuclear energy. Open sources indicate that one nuclear power plant has been constructed in the vicinity of Kirovsk in the central Kola. Construction began early in the 1970s and the first 440,000 kilowatt reactor began production in June 1973. The second was running by early 1975, and there are presently four active reactors working.

MAJOR TOWN AND POPULATION CENTRES.

The eastern part of the Kola is very thinly populated. The population on the peninsula is concentrated in the north-western part, from the Norwegian border to the Murmansk fjord, and along the north-south running corridor from Murmansk to Kandalaksha at the White Sea.

Nikel', very close to the Norwegian border, is a typical mining town at the western end of the nickel-copper formation. Near the eastern end of it we find the town of Zapoljarnyy. To the north-east is the town of Petchenga at the south end of the Petchenga fjord. This town has long traditions as an important port for the Soviet fishing fleet. It is also the nearest harbour for the nickel-copper mining area to the south-west.

Several roads and a railroad connect the north-west to the heavily populated Murmansk fjord area to the east. The fjord-interspersed coastline north of this area, between Murmansk and Petchenga, is exclusively a military naval basing area with large population concentrations. Major bases include Polyarnyy at the entrance to the Kol'skiy Zaliv, and further south and on the eastern side of the fjord, Severomorsk, once an important civil harbour, and today the main naval base on the Kola and peacetime Headquarters of the Northern Fleet.

Somewhat to the south, the linked harbour complexes of Seleny-Mys and Murmansk stretch out in the north-south direction along the eastern flank of the fjord. These are combined civil-military areas,

with Murmansk serving as the main harbour for the Atlantic fishing fleet. It also contains the main canneries of the Murmansk *oblast* fish industry as well as freezing plants and other types of food industry. There are shipyards, machine building and metal work factories, production centres for building materials, woodworking and textile industries.

Further south along the fjord, where it turns into the Tuloma River, are the smaller towns of Kola and Murmashi, mainly providing supporting services for Murmansk. The town of Kola is situated on the top of the communications lines leading southwards. From this point the main road and rail links to Leningrad lead through a narrow industrial and population area in the centre of the Kola, running through the steep mountains by Monchegorsk and Kirovsk and on to Kandalaksha at the south-western-most edge of the Kola.

The new mining towns of Olenegorsk and Monchegorsk are sited along this central communication link, almost in the centre of the Kola Peninsula. In this area, in addition to the mining activity mentioned earlier, there are very large chemical industries and hydro-electrical power plants, and a number of secondary industries. In the town of Kirovsk for instance, the apatite mining resulted in the establishment of production units for building materials. This area has been considerably built up over the last few decades. Thus the town of Apatity nearly doubled its population from 1959 to 1967 (20,000 to 38,000).

The town of Kandalaksha has the innermost harbour of the White Sea, and is an important communications centre for the connections between Murmansk and Leningrad, and eastward along the southern coast of the Kola Peninsula. Kandalaksha has a diverse industry that includes metallurgical, building material and woodworking factories. The important process of refining alumina to aluminium is done in Kandalaksha.

Generally the combined increase in civil and military activity in the Kola region is also reflected in the population growth. Though the statistics are far from satisfactory, the growth of Murmansk may be assumed to represent the general trend here. According to the 1959 census for the Murmansk *oblast*, the populations of the four largest towns were:

Murmansk	220,000
Monchegorsk	46,000
Kirovsk	39,000
Kandalaksha	37,000

The growth of Murmansk alone between 1959 and 1979 is shown in the following table:

Year	1959	1967	1970	1974	1979
Population	222,000	287,000	309,000	347,000	381,000

CHAPTER 9

The Physical Geography and Climate of the Kola Peninsula

JOHNNY SKORVE

The elongated Kola Peninsula stretches to the south-east from the north-east parts of Norway and Finland. Geologically it consists of very old Archaen rocks, mainly granites and gneiss. In the north-west, the coast is cut by several fjords lying approximately perpendicular to the coastline, with the Kolskiy Zaliv, leading into Murmansk, by far the largest and longest. The western part of the Kola is characterised by gentle landforms that reach up to an altitude of 650 metres above sea level (masl). The whole peninsula is dominated by the glacial sculpturing of the landscape during the recent ice ages. There are many lakes in the western part of Kola. From the outer part of the Murmansk fjord there is a 'corridor' of lowland running southward along the Murmansk, Olenegorsk, Kandalaksha line.

Most of the corridor between Olenegorsk and Kandalaksha is occupied by the large Lake Imandra, 130 masl. South of the long Lake Notozero and west of Olenegorsk there are three mountains all with summits very close to 1000 masl. Between the two lakes, Imandra and Umbozero, is the Khrebet Khibiny mountain formation with its tallest peak 1290 masl, which is also the highest point on the Kola Peninsula. East of Lake Umbozero is the Lovozerskiye Tundra Mountains that reach up to 1170 masl. Further to the south and south-east the topography is less pronounced, with hills between 650 and 400 masl. From here the landscape gets even more gentle with gradually lower terrain as it approaches the northern shore of the White Sea.

One 400 metre high elongated hill does run somewhat inland but this is parallel to the north-east coastline of the peninsula.

On the south and south-east part of Kola there are long ridges, consisting of morainic drift and so called glacifluvial material, that are themselves parallel and also parallel with the southern coastline about thirty kilometres further south. These ridges were formed about 10,000 years ago, as deposits near the margin of the melting ice sheet, at the end of the last ice age. It started about 80,000 years ago when snow and ice started to accumulate in the Scandinavian mountains. At the peak of glaciation most of northern Europe was covered by ice several thousand metres thick.

Today several lakes on Kola have formed behind these morainic ridges. Very similar glacial deposits of even greater size are found in south Finland as the Salpausselkä and the Ra-ridges in south-east Norway, both are of the same age as those on the Kola Peninsula.

THE CLIMATE

Murmansk, with more than 380,000 inhabitants, is the world's largest city north of the Arctic circle, and it is still growing. The importance of climate is obvious in the growth of Murmansk to its present size, and for the increased activity on Kola as a whole.

THE BARENTS SEA

The Barents Sea covers an area of 1.6 million square kilometres and has an average depth of 400 metres. Its water volume is 500,000 cubic kilometres, which is ten times that of the North Sea. The Barents Sea is the key to the climate of the Kola Peninsula and its surroundings. Proximity to the ocean in this part of the world generally means a mild winter and a rather cold summer. This rule is valid for the Kola just as it is for the long Norwegian coast to the west.

Westerly winds over the Barents Sea bring most of the 400 to 450 millimetres a year precipitation. The number of days when precipitation occurs number about 200 to 250. Most of the rain falls in the spring while in the autumn rain is more rare. In the winter rain only occurs during thaws. As a whole, snowfall is somewhat more frequent than rain, and cloudy skies occur for more than 80 per cent of the year.

The climate of the Kola Peninsula and northern Scandinavia is far from what could be expected when parts of the region are situated north of the 70th parallel. However Scandinavia is strongly favoured by the relatively warm Gulf Stream water that moves along the Norwegian coast towards the north east. The Gulf Stream water continues further east and also in the south-east direction along the north facing coast

of Kola. However the Gulf Stream effect decreases eastward as the warm water gradually is marked with considerably colder water in the Barents Sea. Thus the climate in the north eastern part of Kola is a lot harsher than further west.

Oceanographic measurements off the northern coast of Kola show that there are no big differences between the summer and winter water temperatures. In August the western Kola coastal waters have a temperature of 9.5 degrees Centigrade, while in the central area the temperature is 8.6 degrees Centigrade, and 7.5 degrees Centigrade just east of Gremikha. Late February coastal water temperatures

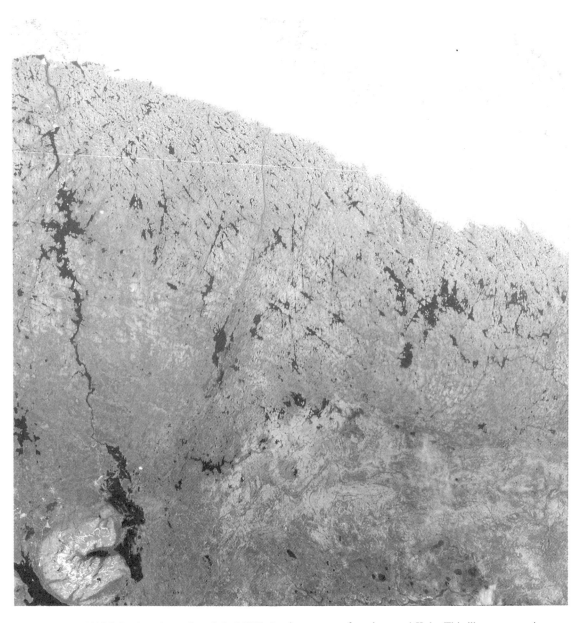

PLATE 9.1. MSS-5 *Landsat* picture from July 4 1985 showing an area of north central Kola. This illustrates a quite frequent situation during periods with fair weather in the summer. In the upper part of the picture coastal fog is seen drifting in from the sea. However it is only obscuring a few kilometres beyond the coastline. By comparing this picture with Plate 9.3 from June 5th 1986 of the same area, it is obvious that only the land with close proximity to the coastline is obscured by fog. Near the lower left corner is the 1170 metre tall Lovozerskiye Tundra mountain, between the two lakes Umbozero and Lovozero. There is still some snow left in the highest part of the mountain. (Photo NASA)

PLATE 9.2. MSS-5 *Landsat* picture from March 24th 1980 covering 177 × 182 kilometres of the north-eastern Kola showing the snow-covered landscape close to the end of a long winter. Near the centre is the sharp Cape Sswatoi Nos peninsula and just below, to the left of it, the new strategic ballistic missile submarine base at Gremikha sheltered to the North by some small islands. On the right hand side of the picture the western flank of the winter polar ice stands out clearly. From it a swarm of small ice rafts are drifting along the coast in the direction of Cape Sswatoi Nos. On its sheltered western shore some ice has formed and also on the lee side of the island, north of Kremikha. The black line on the left is due to a fault caused by the satellites imaging instrument. (Photo NASA)

off Petchenga, Murmansk, the central coast and east of Gremikha are respectively 3.1, 1.7, 0.3 and −1.1 degrees Centigrade. These temperatures clearly show that the effect of the Gulf Stream warming the Barents Sea is evident during the summer as well as in the winter. Just east of the new strategic ballistic missile submarine base at Gremikha, the long north pointing peninsula, Cape Sswatoi Nos, forms a climatic dividing line. To the west of this feature the coast is ice-free during the winter whilst further east sea ice appears frequently as the influence of the eastern polar region begins to öminate.

In the Murmansk area January is milder than on the northern coast of the Caspian Sea. The White Sea to the south of the Kola Peninsula has a colder climate than the Barents Sea. This is especially predominant in the winter and depends on the degree to which the sea freezes.

The strongly moderating effect of the Gulf Stream is indicated by the fact that the winter temperatures along the Kola seaboard are ten to fifteen degrees Centigrade higher than in other parts of the Soviet Union at the same latitude. The fjords on the northern coast of the Kola are thereby normally kept ice-free during the whole winter, which is of the uttermost importance for the very large naval fleet stationed here.

However, the summer temperatures on Kola do not differ much from other northern areas of the Soviet Union. Close to the coast, the July temperature is nine to ten degrees Centigrade. Further inland, the summers are somewhat warmer. During high pressure situations, the daily high can climb to between twenty and thirty degrees Centigrade. The difference between the coastal and inland zones is clearly reflected by the distribution of vegetation. Close to the coast, the terrain is bare with no, or very scanty vegetation. Further inland, the vegetation has a more sheltered environment and here we find a true moss and lichen cover, while other parts have draft scrub and birch forest (Betula Nana). There is no continuous permafrost on Kola.

The climate in the Murmansk area (68 degrees 58′N, 33 degrees 03′E) is reflected in the following table with monthly temperatures and precipitation in degrees Centigrade and millimetres:

	JAN	FEB	MAR	APR	MAY	JUN	JUL	AUG	SEPT	OCT	NOV	DEC
C	−10.1	−10.5	−6.5	−1.4	3.5	9.6	12.9	11.5	6.2	0.6	−4.8	−8.1
mm	25.3	15.0	17.2	17.5	21.5	43.3	70.0	62.5	44.6	32.7	35.6	25.2

AVERAGE ANNUAL TEMPERATURE: 0.2 degrees Centigrade

AVERAGE TOTAL ANNUAL PRECIPITATION: 410.5 mm

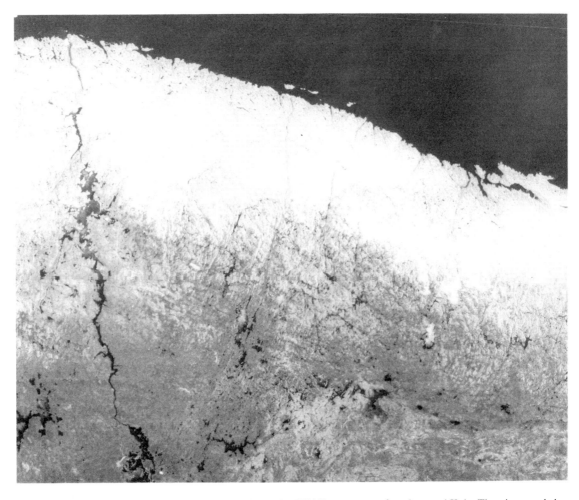

PLATE 9.3. MSS-5 *Landsat* picture from June 5th 1986 showing 147 × 177 kilometre area of north central Kola. The winter cooled water in the Barents Sea warms more slowly than the air and its influence on the coastal zone results in late melting of snow and lake ice. On this picture the white coastal zone stands out clearly in contrast to the snowfree landscape to the south of it. (Photo NASA)

THE SEASONS

In northern areas like Kola the air temperature is used to differentiate between the four seasons of the year. The period when the average daily air temperature stays below freezing (zero degrees Centigrade) is defined as winter. Spring is the time it takes the average air temperature to rise from zero degrees Centigrade to ten degrees Centigrade, while the summer is defined as the period when the average temperature stays above ten degrees Centigrade. The autumn is represented by the time it takes the temperature to drop from ten degrees Centigrade to zero degrees Centigrade. During April and May spring becomes the dominating season with snow melting and the break up of ice taking place.

The warming of the Barents Sea water is much slower than the spring rise in air temperature. This has a pronounced effect by slowing down the melting rate of ice and snow in the coastal areas and particularly in areas of still, cold water. The influence of this thermal inertia decreases with distance from the sea and is reflected by the timing of the transition from spring to summer. In the central part of Kola the summer starts between 15th June and the 20th June and on the coast between the Norwegian–Soviet border and Murmansk the date is July 1st. In the northeast part of the Kola the starting point is well into the month of July and here the summer lasts only a few weeks. On the northern coast of Kola the summer ends around August 15th and ten days later further south. In the central part of the peninsula winter starts on November 1st and in the coastal areas about 15 days later.

The vegetation in an area can be looked upon as an expression of the climate. The growing season takes place when the average air temperature stays above three degrees Centigrade. In the south-west of Kola the growing season begins in the period May 20th to 25th and is at its peak around June 1st. In the Nikel'–Murmansk area it starts around June 5th, on the Poluostrov Bybacky June 10th and in north-east Kola even later. The western part of the Kola has the longest growing season and along the line from Nikel' to Kandelaksha it lasts 110 days. In north-west Kola the growing season ends around September 25th.

Glossary of Terms

1. Soviet Administrative Commands.

A. *High Administrative Commands.*

Abbreviation	*Soviet Term*	*Translation*
SO	*Sovjet Oborony*	Defence Council

This is the highest military-economic planning body, responsible for preparing the USSR for war.[1]

GVS	*Glavnyy Voyenyy Sovjet*	Ministry of Defence[2]
GVS-KMO	*GVS-Kollegiya Ministerstva Oborony*	Collegium of the Ministry of Defence

Responsible to the SO for the training and readiness of the armed forces.[3]

GS	*General'nyy Shtab*	General Staff

Peacetime executive agency for the GVS-KMO.[4]

n.a.	n.a.	Commanders-in-Chief of the five services and the airborne troops.

Responsible for the development of the respective services.[5]

B. *Services and Arms of Service.*[6]

Abbreviation	*Soviet Term*	*Translation*
RVSN	*Raketnyye Vojska Strategicheskovo Naznachenija*	Strategic Rocket Forces
SV	*Sukhoputnyye Vojska*	Ground Forces
TV	Tankovyye Vojska	Tank Troops
MV	Motostrelkovyye Vojska	Motorised Troops
RViA	Raketnyye Vojska i Artillerija	Rocket Troops and Artillery
VVPO	Vojska Vojskovoj Protovovozdushnoj Oborony	Troops of Troop Air Defence
VPVO	*Vojska Protovovozdushnoy Oborony*	Troops of Air Defence
APVO	Aviatsija Protivovozdushnoy Oborony	Aviation of Air Defence

ZRV	Zenitnyye Raketnyye Vojska	Zenith Rocket Troops
RTV	Radioteckhnicheskije Vojska	Radio-Technical Troops
PKO	Protivokosmicheskaya Oborona[7]	Antispace Defence
PRO	Protivoraketnaya Oborna[8]	Antirocket Defence
VVS	*Voyenno Vozdushnyye Sily*	The Air Forces
DA	Dal'nyaja Aviatsija	Long Range Aviation
FA	Frontovaja Aviatsija	Frontal Aviation
VTA	Voyenno-Transportnaja Aviatsija	Transport Aviation
AA	Armeijskaja Aviatsija	Army Aviation
VMF	*Voyenno-Morskoj Flot*	The Navy
PL	Podvodnaja Lodkha	Submarines
AVMF	Aviatsija Vojenno-Morskogo Flota	Naval Aviation
K	Korabl'	Surface Vessels
MP	Morskaja Pekhota[9]	Naval Infantry
VDV	*Vozdushno-Desantnyye Vojska*	

C. Regional Command

Abbreviation	Soviet Term	Translation
VO	*Voyennyy Okrug*	Military District

Regional administrative command responsible for the support, training, materiel and readiness of all armed forces within its district.[10]

2. Soviet Operational Commands.

Abbreviation	Soviet Term	Translation
GKO	*Gosudarstvennyy Komitet Oborony*	State Committee of Defence

This is the highest civilian-military operational command organ. It is composed of the General Secretary of the CPSU, the Minister of Defence, the Chief of the General Staff, the Chairman of the KGB, the Chairman of the Council of Ministers of the Soviet Union. In addition other individuals may be called in as needed.[11]

VGK	*Verkhovni Glavnokomandovanie*	Supreme High Command

This is the highest military command, and there is only one such post.[12]

GS	*General'nyy Shtab*	General Staff

Wartime support agency for the VGK.[13]

GK	*Glavnoe Komandovanie*	High Command

These are the second highest ranking operational commands, headed by Commanders-in-Chief. There are six High Commands at present, controlling the two main services responsible for global strategic nuclear operations (GK of the Strategic Nuclear Forces and GK of the Vojska PVO) and the four main theatre-level groupings of forces (Western, South-western Far Eastern and Southern).[14]

n.a.	n.a.	Special VGK representative.

These are created by the VGK and allocated according to circumstances. They have an equal or higher rank to the GK theatre commands and are assigned to assist the commander of a strategically vital operation. Thus this 'VGK Assistance

Command' could be assigned to a Front or even an Army, if the operations of that formation were judged sufficiently important.[15]

n.a.   n.a.   Commanders of the forces directly subordinated to the VGK.

This is generally speaking the third highest ranking command level in the Soviet command structure. There are at least seven such commands, consisting of two detached Fronts, one detached Fleet, and four special arms of service: the theatre bomber forces, the airborne divisions, the military transport aviation and the strategic reserve.[16]

K   *Komandoyuschii*   Command Council

These command the Front operations. They consist of the Military Commander of the Front forces (Chairman), the Head of the Political Directorate of that Front or Army District, the First Party Secretary of the Republic or Province in which the unit is operating, and the First Deputy Commander Chief of Staff.[17]

Stavka   This is a headquarters command group assisting the commander of the unit at that particular level. Thus there is a Stavka VGK, Stavka GK, etc.[18]

TVD   *Teatr Voennykh Deistvii*   Theatre of Strategic Military Action

The world is divided into at least sixteen such territorial entities, including land areas (TVD), oceanic areas (OTVD) and maritime areas (MTVD). Not to be confused with the GK TVD which is an entirely different concept.[19]

PLARB   *Podvodnaya Lodka Atomnaya*   Ballistic Missile Submarine[20]
                        Raketnaya Ballisticheskaya

Notes

1. POLMAR, Norman, *Guide to the Soviet Navy*. Annapolis, Naval Institute Press, 3rd. ref. ed., 1983; p. 7.

   SCOTT, Harriet Fast and William F.; *The Armed Forces of the USSR*. London, Arms and Armour Press, 3rd. rev. ed., 1984; pp. 105–108.

2. SCOTT, op. cit., p. 108.

3. ibid., pp. 108–111.

   POLMAR, op. cit., p. 7.

4. SUVOROV, Viktor: 'Strategic Command and Control. The Soviet approach.' *International Defense Review*, vol. 17, No. 12, December 1984: pp. 1818–1820.

   POLMAR, op. cit., p. 7.

5. SCOTT, op. cit., pp. 141–182, 191.

6. Unless otherwise stated all terms are from:

   SCOTT and SCOTT: *The Armed Forces . . .*, op. cit., pp. 141–178.

7. SCOTT, William F.: 'The Soviets and Strategic Defense.' *Air Force Magazine*, Vol. 69, N. 3, March 1986: p. 44.

8. ibid., p. 44.

9. POLMAR, Norman: *Guide to the Soviet Navy*. Annapolis, United States Naval Institute Press, 3rd. rev. ed., 1982: p. 29.

10. ibid., pp. 185, 192.

11. HINES, John G. and Phillip A. PETERSEN: 'Changing the Soviet System of Control.' *International Defense Review*, Vol. 19, No. 3, March 1986: p. 286.

    POLMAR, Norman: *Guide to the Soviet Navy*. Annapolis, Naval Institute Press, 3rd. rev. ed., 1983: p. 7.

    SCOTT, Harriet Fast and William F.: *The Armed Forces of the USSR*. London, Arms and Armour Press, 3rd. rev. ed., 1984: pp. 105–108, 122.

    SUVOROV, Viktor: *Inside the Soviet Army*. London, Hamish Hamilton, 1st. ed., 1982: pp. 32–35.

12. SUVOROV, Viktor: 'Strategic Command and Control. The Soviet approach.' *International Defense Review*, Vol. 17, No. 12, December 1984: pp. 1815–1816.

13. SCOTT, Harriet Fast and William F.: *The Armed Forces of the USSR*. London, Arms and Armour, 3rd. rev. ed., 1984: pp. 111, 115.

    SUVOROV, Viktor: 'Strategic Command and Control. The Soviet approach.' *International Defense Review*, vol. 17, No. 12, December 1984: pp. 1818–1820.

    POLMAR, op. cit., p. 7.

14. SUVOROV: 'Strategic Command . . .', op. cit., pp. 1818–1820.

15. SUVOROV: 'Strategic Command . . .', op. cit., pp. 1817–1818.

16. SUVOROV: Inside the Soviet Army, op. cit., pp. 36–40.

17. SUVOROV: 'Strategic Command . . .', op. cit., p. 1820.

18. ibid., p. 1820.

19. HINES and PETERSEN: 'Changing . . .', op. cit., pp. 281–289.

    HINES, John G. and Phillip A. PETERSEN: 'Is NATO Thinking too Small? A comparison of command structures.' *International Defense Review*, Vol. 19, No. 5, May 1986: pp. 563–572.

    SUVOROV: 'Strategic Command . . .', op. cit., pp. 1813–1815.

20. POLMAR: *Guide to . . .*, op. cit., p. 6.